Babbling Corpse

Vaporwave and the
Commodification of Ghosts

T0167562

Babbling Corpse

Vaporwave and the Commodification of Ghosts

Grafton Tanner

Winchester, UK
Washington, USA

JOHN HUNT PUBLISHING

First published by Zero Books, 2016
Zero Books is an imprint of John Hunt Publishing Ltd., Laurel House, Station Approach,
Alresford, Hants, SO24 9JH, UK
office1@jhpbooks.net
www.johnhuntpublishing.com
www.zero-books.net

For distributor details and how to order please visit the 'Ordering' section on our website.

Text copyright: Grafton Tanner 2015

ISBN: 978 1 78279 759 3
Library of Congress Control Number: 2015952170

A CIP catalogue record for this book is available from the British Library.

Design: Lapiz Digital Serivices

Printed and bound by CPI Group (UK) Ltd, Croydon, CR0 4YY, UK

We operate a distinctive and ethical publishing philosophy in
all areas of our business, from our global network of authors to
production and worldwide distribution.

CONTENTS

Where there was once the 'real,' there is now only the electronic generation and circulation of almost supernatural simulations. Where there was once stable human consciousness, there are now only the ghosts of fragmented, decentered, and increasingly schizophrenic subjectivities. Where there once was 'depth' and 'affect,' there is now only 'surface.' Where there was once 'meaning,' 'history,' and a solid realm of 'signifieds,' there is now only a haunted landscape of vacant and shifting signifiers.
– *Jeffrey Sconce*[1]

America! / Everything has its price; nearly everything has been bought.
– *Terrance Hayes*[2]

Introduction

Ghostly Encounters

As a teenager, I frequented the "online cinematheque" known as MUBI (formerly The Auteurs) to discuss the art of cinema with like-minded movie lovers and rank my favorite films, hoping to strike up a chat with a prominent critic or filmmaker. The site was welcoming and never exclusive, a space for cinephiles to indulge in everything from listing our favorite Criterion Collection releases to watching and appreciating obscure and neglected films. Everyone heard the other's voice, and opinions were acknowledged and debated fairly and openly. It was my first experience enjoying the "social" part of social media and understanding the extraordinary benefits of being connected with any person on the planet via the Internet.

Late one night, as I trawled through the message boards and left behind scattered comments here and there, I noticed an unfamiliar member was commenting after every one of my posts. I clicked on the member's profile only to discover a blank biography section, no profile picture, and no rated films. The comments underneath my own were always the same – a grainy, lo-res photograph of a middle-aged man with brown hair in midturn towards the camera with the caption, "This is what baked shit looks like," just below it. The blankness of the man's expression combined with the anonymity of the profile shook me up, but what gripped me with an urgent, sudden fear was the fact that this trolling presence had attached itself to me and was posting this photograph and caption after every one of my own posts I made that late night.

Part of the Internet's strangeness stems from the anonymity and pseudonymity it can offer, even as it also allows anyone unprecedented access to the private lives of others. My encounter with this Internet troll on MUBI unsettled me because of its anonymous precision. It commented too soon after my own posts. Its message was always the same. Suddenly I didn't feel like I was in the presence of real people on this website but like I was communicating with their surrogates, their avatars, uncanny copies sent in advance of the real things. I realized the true nature of communication on MUBI and then even more so when I joined Facebook and other social media sites that can offer equal amounts of pseudo- and anonymity. Even before my run-in with the troll, I had not once had communication with any real person on those MUBI message boards. Night after night, I had been sitting in my house in front of my computer with no one else.

It is a confounding and eerie sensation to feel social while alone, thronged with invisible entities whose presence is felt yet who appear wholly absent. These entities are our twenty-first-century ghosts, shorn from their corporeal shells and set loose to glide through cyberspace at lightning speed and with startling precision. We call to one another in the darkness of the Internet, reuniting with hosts of friends and followers, but the act is all theater. There is nothing there in the dark except the dead gaze of a copy.

Western culture teems with so many ghosts: digital doppelgängers, anonymous commenters, and of course the ghosts of our past – the remnants of history, national trauma, and our individual memories, which are more drawn to the sirens of the past in the Information Age than ever before. The digital ghosts, the ghosts in our machines, remind us our technological creations are anything but infallible, yet we become profoundly unnerved when our creations act seemingly with a will of their own. Or, when we encounter a virtual presence whose materiality is anonymous (like the MUBI profile). The ubiquity of digital technology and the desperate faith in technological redemption de-center the human as the locus of experience in history, and this thought is difficult to grasp. When faced with the possible existence of a ghost, a malfunction in ordered normality, we retreat in abject fear. We live in the manufactured illusion that we are still separate from our media extensions when in fact we are interlopers stumbling through a spectral world not for us.

The other ghost resides not in the machine but instead glides over history, loudly declaring its arrival as it reminds us of our forgotten pasts and lost futures, our mutual traumas and former experiences as a Western society. I will touch on both ghostly forms in this book, and I will examine contemporary art and philosophy to better understand why these hauntings occur more frequently in twenty-first-century culture.

At the crux of our haunted culture is vaporwave, an Internet-born electronic-music microgenre that consistently divides critics and listeners alike with its singularly strange aesthetic and guerrilla methods of production. Although it has its roots in avant-garde electronic pioneers such as John Cage and culture jammers like the San Francisco band Negativland, vaporwave as a proper genre and scene emerged only in the early 2010s, and in just a few years it has prompted furious online debate. All the while the scene itself has grown tremendously in a short time, and one could attribute this to both vaporwave's appeal and the ease with which it can be created (more on this later).

Largely ignored by the mainstream press, vaporwave has instead flourished on websites such as Bandcamp and SoundCloud and on Reddit, where a popular subreddit is dedicated solely to discovering new producers and sharing the images and sounds of this nascent yet prolific genre. Because vaporwave exists almost entirely outside the sphere of PR and the music industry at large, it has tremendous "underground" appeal. Here is an entire community of artists, musicians, remixers, and critics listening to and creating strange and justifiably unnerved by floating furniture, sudden chills that come from nowhere, and disembodied voices. These animated objects are uncanny because they rob the familiar of its comfort. There exists a gap between a sound heard and the sound's source, and as audio theorist David Toop notes, "In every place that feels or becomes uncanny and unhomely, there is a sound that does not belong, an interloper."[8] Uncanny sound is phantom sound: it comes into familiarity from nowhere.

But how does one act in the presence of the uncanny? How does the uncanny disrupt our experience of the world? In *The Memory of Place: A Phenomenology of the Uncanny*, Dylan Trigg sets out to accurately describe our experience of memory in terms of spatiality. Writing in the vein of phenomenologists like Gaston Bachelard and Maurice Merleau-Ponty, Trigg asserts that our memories function like the spaces that we used to frequent or even inhabit. The physical dimensions of a childhood home are important in shaping my memory of childhood because I experienced it. Experience and place are intertwined, allowing my memory to form from a particular feeling of childhood as well as a particular place. Trigg is especially interested in the ghosts of these memory houses and the feelings we get upon revisiting a place of memory. For Trigg, experience itself has a lot to do with the "strangeness of things."[9] He writes that "Such an estrangement from the natural world is, I would argue, at the heart of phenomenology."[10] Trigg writes of the "creeping strangeness" that accompanies an encounter with "*augmented familiarity*" (his italics).[11] The uncanny is both old and new, familiar and eerie, and confuses us upon first encounter. We find it "*in the manifold space between experience and thought, perfectly at ease with its ability to invoke repulsion and allure in the subject experiencing the uncanny*" (also his italics).[12] In this gap lies a truly alien realm wherein the strangeness of the everyday rises up to present us with the unalterable reality that the world is not for us.

These gaps produce the ghosts that film theorist Linda Badley refers to in her book. Their very intermediary nature confounds us as they rise from within the familiar to assert its strangeness. Our reaction to such a ghostly encounter would likely resemble Jack Gladney's in Don DeLillo's suburban thriller *White Noise*, when he unexpectedly sees his wife Babette on television. The passage is worth quoting at length:

The face on the screen was Babette's. Out of our mouths came a silence as wary and deep as an animal growl. Confusion, fear, astonishment spilled from our faces. What did it mean? What was she doing there, in black and white, framed in formal borders? Was she dead, missing, disembodied? Was this her spirit, her secret self, some two-dimensional facsimile released by the power of technology, set free to glide through wavebands, through energy levels, pausing to say good-bye to us from the fluorescent screen?

A strangeness gripped me, a sense of psychic disorientation. It was her all right, the face, the hair, the way she blinks in rapid twos and threes. I'd seen her just an hour ago, eating eggs, but her appearance on the screen made me think of her as some distant figure from the past, some ex-wife and absentee mother, a walker in the mists of the dead. If she was not dead, was I? A two-syllable infantile cry, *ba-ba*, issued from the deeps of my soul...[13]

Gladney's description is one of awe and terror, not unlike the emotions felt by the Freelings and their team of parapsychologists when they successfully contact Carol Anne in *Poltergeist*. Jack is reduced to an infantile state, muttering his wife's nickname more as a childlike gurgle than an affectionate gesture. His behavior is that of a person encountering the living dead, witnessing the animation of the inanimate. The familiarity of his wife and his television set turn inside out; his mind cannot properly correlate the information he is given. He confronts the uncanny and undergoes emotional reorientation as he attempts to understand his there-but-not-there wife and the in-betweenness of it all. Babette is an intermediary being, a ghost rising from the spectral glow of the television – present yet absent.

To witness a "haunted" electronic medium is to confront the uncanny with all its gaps. When we listen to a warped vinyl record or examine the visual traces on the blank screen of a finicky television, we are immediately struck by the characteristics of their ghostliness because their malfunction, actual or perceived, indicates a rift between them and their carried messages. The horror then arises from electronic media's propensity to glitch and malfunction, throwing us (the users) into a sudden state of disarray. The analog electronic media of prior decades were particularly prone to presenting ghosts. Unlike the sleek, liquid form of digital media, early radio and television for instance channeled information through a low-definition interface, while static and poor resolution interrupted the flow of sound and image. When the radio signal gives out and another channel comes through cloaked in fuzz and static, it is as if the radio has acted entirely on its own and, most unsettlingly, is more prone to malfunction than maybe we think.

Like ghostly objects of haunted lore, faulty electronic media resemble autonomous interfaces because they seem to operate freely or by the hand of some unseen presence with minimal human interaction involved. Instead of extending the nervous system, as Marshall McLuhan affirms, haunted electronic media appear to transcend the nervous system, and this transcendence suggests that haunted media, such as the television or the radio, are "capable of generating their own autonomous spirit worlds."[14] In other words, these media seem haunted by "ghosts" that dwell within the electronics. Ghosts, as Linda Badley writes, "empty 'reality' of meaning…They are like Derridean words; they 'kill' meaning. Ghosts pretend to assert transcendence but actually speak the nothingness, the death, of the things they name."[15] Here, Badley binds Cixous' assertion of the uncanny with Jacques Derrida's meaningless words to illustrate ghosts as gaps in the meaning of reality signified. They are meaninglessness made manifest. Thus, the television, the phonograph, and the radio all have the propensity to seem infested with "ghosts" and are portrayed as such in fiction and films (like *Poltergeist*) because they remediate information. These types of media assert gaps between the information they relay and their electronic forms, providing the feeling that some unseen force animates them.

Re-Animating the Dead

With the invention of the electronic musical sampler, gaps and remediation took new forms. Now, recorded music could easily be manipulated to create new pieces of music, and entire songs could be constructed solely out of audio samples shorn of context and reference. It was the ultimate postmodern musical gesture and one that proved legally problematic if a sample of an artist's song was used without permission. Music critic Simon Reynolds describes sampling as "a mixture of time-travel and séance" and characterizes it as "the musical art of ghost coordination and ghost arrangement."[16] Reynolds' choice of ghostly metaphors when describing the capabilities of the sampler is apt; the previously static recordings of artists from any era could now be rearranged in endless ways. A 1970s disco hit could be joined with a Charles Mingus tune to create an ahistorical piece of music, giving new life to "dead" records. It is Franken-music, using various pieces of former wholes to create a new being.

The sampler is still used by artists today for both in-studio recording and live performance, but the software sampler and the digital audio workstation (DAW) now allow musicians to easily produce sampled music directly on their computers.

Before DAWs became relatively inexpensive or even free to acquire, artists creating appropriated forms of music relied on phonographs, tape machines, cassette players, and the sampler to produce samples. The ease with which someone with a BitTorrent client can now pirate an expensive DAW, such as Ableton Live, enables anyone with a computer to produce amateur or perhaps professional-grade sampled music. Most DAWs come equipped with some kind of sampler, so the average DJ, producer, sound artist, or amateur can not only load and manipulate samples in a DAW but also mix and master those tracks. The end result can be a professional-grade music track produced solely on a laptop by anyone.

But the art of sampling problematizes the notions of authorship and source originality and magnifies recorded music's association with the uncanny to an extreme degree. Writing prior to the invention of the modern hardware sampler, Marshall McLuhan categorizes various media and their respective transcendence of certain "walls." The phonograph, in particular, can be thought of as the "music hall without walls" for McLuhan.[17] Armed with this terminology, the sampler can be considered the studio or perhaps the phonograph without "walls." The phonograph drags sound and music outside the music venue, and the sampler takes the track of recorded music outside the phonograph and into a mechanism that has the ability to rework that track into a new form. What about the DAW? Perhaps McLuhan would consider the DAW a sampler without "walls," indicating a truly wall-less medium capable of producing endless sound and allowing musicians to sample anything with the push of a button.

Such an ability to render endless loops accentuates the art of sampling's relationship with the uncanny and, more specifically, the idea of haunted media. As an art form of remediation and appropriation, sampling requires an artist to transpose media onto different media, and the creation of

7

songs by sampling other recorded sound clips exposes gaps: gaps in authorship, continuity, and the information needed to determine originality. The sampler can also appear haunted because of its technological capability to loop samples and songs for an innumerable duration. The phonograph can allow music to play with only the initial touch of a "play" button, but eventually, the vinyl record ends – and so does the music. However, software and hardware samplers enable users to create and distort any loop of any sound for any length of time.

One of the defining characteristics of many vaporwave tracks is this element of repetition, which draws attention to the uncanniness of audio looping. Usually focusing on one fragment of an entire song, a vaporwave producer will then loop that fragment *ad nauseum*, often for the length of the entire track. The effect is absurd, hilarious, unnerving, and sometimes boring. Can you really sit through a three-minute song built from a fifteen-second loop repeated twelve times? The repetition in songs by MACINTOSH PLUS, INTERNET CLUB, and Local News are meant to be exhaustive and to walk that fine line between funny and uncanny, and listening to an entire track can waver between transcendental elation and disengaged ennui.

This emotional mixture of unease and humor, boredom and profundity, likely stems from our detestation of repetitive gestures. In her book *On Repeat: How Music Plays the Mind*, Elizabeth Hellmuth Margulis ascribes this aversion to repetition to "the idea that thoughts are not our own, spontaneous, soul-engendered entities, but rather products of some invisible, subconscious script," and likens our distrust to "a fear about automaticity and loss of control."[18] Her example is HAL 9000 in Stanley Kubrick's *2001: A Space Odyssey*. As astronaut Dave Bowman shuts down the sentient supercomputer, HAL repeats the phrase *"I can feel it"* in a flat, unemotional voice, quite unlike his calm yet rational manner of speaking heard until that point in the film.[19] Repetition means mechanical processes are underway. For the human, repetition spells a loss of humanity in favor of the machine. A shuddering, repeating machine such as the dying HAL 9000 presents us with an animated corpse ventriloquized by some unseen force. Perhaps for humans, we fear not the mechanization and loss of control so much as the fear of becoming Frankenstein's monster – a babbling corpse, hollow yet able to run amok with machinelike skill. Barely sentient, yet functioning all too well. Again, Simon Reynolds provides an apt metaphor with the stigmatized broomsticks in Disney's *The Sorcerer's Apprentice*, in which the multiplying, spellbound brooms become "an ungodly slave swarm dementedly fetching water and causing a flood."[20] There is a horror here in the proliferation and constantly reproducing throng of sentient objects. They are nonhuman, autonomous, unconscious, and eerily precise in their repetitions.

A great deal of vaporwave's unsettling sound comes from the relentless repetition of vocal hooks, introductory motifs, and refrains (among other samples of song sections). A good example is "Sports Champions" by Local News in which the line "Here's to the winners…" is repeated for nearly its entire 3:42 running time. At a certain point, the voice loses its immediacy and no longer sounds like the familiar voice of Frank Sinatra. Eventually, Sinatra's lyric becomes a sound bite, a mechanized voice repeating the same meaningless line without ever arriving at a resolution. "Sports Champions" is the sound of a song trying to find its footing and never escaping the circular dungeon of the intro. Instead, I find it funny that Sinatra is stuck on a loop, cheers-ing the "winners" until the congratulatory gesture is rendered vapid; but the effect can also be quite disturbing, as if the CD is skipping, the vinyl is warped, or my iTunes is glitching.

"Sports Champions" and many other vaporwave tracks foreground the glitch in their faulty, annoying, and disquieting splendor. Copenhagen University Lecturer Torben Sangild notes that a glitch does not indicate a "collapse of the machinery" but instead cues us into realizing that "something is wrong."[21] Malfunctioning technology, Sangild illustrates, is like a broken hammer: because we are "aware of its construction and design" when it is broken, it "becomes unfamiliar, no longer an unquestioned extension of ourselves."[22] Echoing McLuhan's terms, a defective piece of technology, such as a broken television or a buggy iPhone, is analogous to a faulty nervous system. Our extensions, the technology of our every day, disrupt us almost on a physiological level when they falter, and then we must immediately fix the occurring glitch in order to return to normalcy, stability, and familiarity. Vaporwave is one artistic style that seeks to rearrange our relationship with electronic media by forcing us to recognize the unfamiliarity of ubiquitous technology. Whether it is the sound of skipping audio ("花の専門店" by MACINTOSH PLUS), a warped VHS ("Commercial Dreams" by MIDNIGHT TELEVISION), or a haunted radio ("midnight luvr" by new dreams ltd initiation tape), vaporwave music often tends to emphasize the uncanniness of glitches via repetition or audio effects such as distortion, pitch shifting, and high doses of compression.

Ghosts in the Machine

Another crucial element of vaporwave's haunting aesthetic is its editing, which is often jagged and unexpected. Songs like INTERNET CLUB's "PACIFIC" and "All Night" by MIDNIGHT TELEVISION are comprised of poorly edited samples, and the effect is an accentuation of the artificial means by which the songs were produced. Though not all vaporwave tracks spotlight their editing, many celebrate remediation and amateur sampling as a way to undermine the smooth, professional-grade production heard in mainstream Western popular music. According to Simon Reynolds, this style of intentionally bad sampling "resists and subverts the CGI-style seamlessness that today's sequencing-and-editing music software at once enables and enforces."[23] Vaporwave stands in opposition to the sleek production of contemporary music and can also call attention to the artifice of music production with oddly cut loops (causing the jagged samples to resist turning over on the downbeat of a measure), continuous repetition, and by exposing the audible "click" of the sample looping over in the mix. The ostentatious display of artifice flips the art of sampling on its head; vaporwave artists tend to disregard the invisible editing of mass-produced massively consumed pop fodder.

Vaporwave's glitch aesthetic is particularly eerie, with its cut-and-paste editing and pitch-shifted vocals. This "haunted" quality of the genre's overall sound is perhaps its greatest strength in producing an uncanny emotional response. "In science fiction, ghosts in machines always appear as malfunctions, glitches, interruptions in the normal flow of things," writes cultural theorist Janne Vanhanen.[24] "Through a malfunction, a glitch, we get a fleeting glimpse of an alien intelligence at work."[25] That "alien intelligence" could be the very inside-ness of the machine at hand, the interior workings that remain entirely hidden unless we disassemble the tool and risk facing the uncanny in its destabilizing guise. The ever-working alien world is exposed in the information gaps, which yawn more widely when the machine hiccups and stumbles. These glitches interrupt our expectations while deceiving and annoying us. They undermine our notion of what the machine is supposed to do *for* us, not *without* us. In this way, our electronic machines take on lives of their own and appear capable of functioning perfectly well without humans – a complete transcendence into other-worldly sentience.

The sound of this transformation is best exemplified in the ghostly voices of many vaporwave tracks and eccojams, which are chopped and screwed versions of 80s and 90s soft-rock hits perfected in form by Brooklyn-based artist Daniel Lopatin (of Oneohtrix Point Never). Working under the alias Chuck Person, Lopatin released his *Chuck Person's Eccojams Vol. 1* in 2010 and paved the way for vaporwave's classical period along with proto-vapor pioneer James Ferraro. *Vol. 1* is a collection of these eccojams with source material ranging from "Too Little Too Late" by former teen idol Jojo to Toto's "Africa" (a favorite of many producers to vaporize). Upon first listen, I found myself vacillating between dreadful sadness, hilarity, and angst, as if the very act of my listening defied these maudlin songs and exposed them for the saccharine sham they are. In reality, I enjoy both Jojo and Toto, but these eccojams present the original songs in an alien way, forcing me to reconsider them from a variety of perspectives: as cultural trash, as jokes, as actually beautiful pieces of music. Ultimately, though, *Vol. 1* pushes me to truly *listen* to the voices shorn of mainstream glamour and big-budget glitz. They sound naked and strange, as if they are aware of their presence or being. It is the sound of so many glitches: malfunctioning radio, fuzzy audio, slowed-down LPs. The voices speak through their electronic medium, a true choir of ghosts in the machine, corporeal yet spectral.

Vol. 1 is also cloaked in a strange haze of anonymity, even though the release is openly credited to Daniel Lopatin. On the face of it, the release is disarmingly oblique – why Chuck Person? How many volumes exist? From what wonky radio station are these pop perversions streaming? Which leads me to a larger question: how many people are actually making vaporwave?

It is not uncommon for several vaporwave projects to be credited to one person. Producer Ramona Xavier has released vaporwave music under a variety of aliases: Vektroid, New Dreams Ltd, 情報デスクVIRTUAL, Sacred Tapestry, Laserdisc Visions, fuji grid tv, and esc 不在, to name only a few. The anonymity of vaporwave erases the notion of authorship altogether. In a way, a vaporwave release belongs to the genre at large and not to any one producer, establishing a multifarious genre field that eschews something so totalizing as ownership. Regardless, listening to vaporwave and not knowing its source is quite alienating, especially in a time when the music press fetishizes open-and-closed narratives (think of the rise and end of LCD Soundsystem along with the headline-making Death Grips, which I will discuss in the following chapter). The anonymity is part of the experience of listening to vaporwave. You're engaging with music that comes from nowhere, that can be attributed to no one or at best a faceless moniker, and that resists easy analysis.

There is something strikingly inhuman about all of this – anonymous sources, haunted televisions, uncanny houses, the utter strangeness of the familiar, everyday world. That vaporwave – this enigmatic, twenty-first-century, Internet-born genre – is complicit in foregrounding the eeriness of electronic media and the mundanity of media technologies in contemporary culture is not uncommon. In fact, one could draw a line connecting vaporwave to the fairly recent artistic and philosophical trends that de-center the human being as the locus of all experiences in favor of proposing what philosopher Graham Harman calls an "object-oriented philosophy." As musicians, artists, critics, and philosophers analyze the strangeness of contemporaneity, a startling theme reveals itself: the erasure of humanity's privileged reign.

Chapter 2

Erasing the Human: Anthrodecentrism and Co(s)mic Horror

Nature: Did you think by any chance that the world was made for you alone? Now let me tell you that in my works, laws, and operations, except for very few of them, my purpose was not, and is not, the happiness or unhappiness of men...Finally, even if I happened to wipe out your entire species, I wouldn't notice it.

– Giacomo Leopardi, "Dialogue Between Nature and an Icelander"

The Anthropocene is the era in which man's impact on the earth has become the single force driving change on the planet, thus giving shape to nature, shifting seas, changing the climate, and causing the disappearance of innumerable species, including placing humanity on the brink of extinction.

– Irmgard Emmelhainz

In April 2007, at a conference held at Goldsmiths, University of London, four philosophers sought to undo the past century's philosophical phobia of realism. This group – comprised of Ray Brassier, Iain Hamilton Grant, Graham Harman, and Quentin Meillassoux – gathered together under a singular philosophical term, one that held slightly different meanings for each thinker: speculative realism. Their object of study was Immanuel Kant's philosophy of "correlationism" (termed by Meillassoux), or the privileging of the human as the host for thought. In other words, they endeavored to eliminate the idea of "a mind-independent reality...because the very fact that we are thinking of such a reality means that it is not mind-independent after all."[3]

By correlating the mind with thought, a vicious cycle begins: how can we fathom reality as the bizarre wilderness it is? How can we think of ourselves as just another object in the material universe of objects? How can we think, not as a human, but as just another thing?

This nonhuman turn has alienating ramifications for philosophy (*in dismantling correlationism, do we absolve ourselves of blame?*), but its timeliness seems all the more appropriate when one considers the climate in which it was conceived. Climate, both figuratively and literally here, as I will discuss later. Taken up by philosophers such as Timothy Morton, Eugene Thacker, and Ian Bogost, speculative realism and its constituent term, object-oriented ontology (OOO), mirror the contemporary Western world's fascination with dread as much as they grapple with its material strangeness. With the ever-present threat of human extinction looming overhead, whether perpetuated by the media or rightly warned of by the science community, the speculative realists' words start to ring true.

In a 2014 podcast interview with WNYC's Radiolab, Eugene Thacker and Simon Critchley, both philosophers and professors at The New School, discuss the recent fascination with dread as it relates to Thacker's own book, *In the Dust of This Planet: Horror of Philosophy vol. 1*. In the interview, host Jad Abumrad talks with Thacker about the nihilism and popularity of HBO's dread-noir hit, *True Detective*, and the fashion world's embrace of his book's title, but their primary concern is with today's youth: why are young people so turned on to the idea of meaninglessness? And is this anything new?

"Just turn on the news," Jad says in his conversation with Simon Critchley, and anyone can see the incessant stream of horrors being offered up twenty-four hours a day: beheadings, disease outbreaks, endless war.[4] Not enough horror? Jad also mentions in his interview the specter of global warming, waiting in the wings at history's end to wipe us from the face of the planet. He notes:

...the IPCC – the Inter-governmental Panel on Climate Change – released a report where, for the first time, they stopped using the language of prevention and shifted to the language of adaptation. In other words, hundreds of scientists and policy makers – this is the world's top organization for assessing climate change – were now saying: we can't stop it. It's inevitable.[5]

And finally, there is the youth's overall opinion of the future in general. "In a recent *Wall Street Journal* poll," Jad says, "seventy-six percent of people eighteen and over weren't confident that the future is going to be brighter than the past."[6] Indeed, no future can be imagined when we live in the horror of immediacy with everything afforded to us *right now*, and no planet will exist if capitalism's devastation of the natural order continues unchecked. A common perception (and one that is shared by *True Detective*'s Season One star, the pessimist-cum-mystic Rustin Cohle) is that humans are the problem. Whether we are killing each other, or the planet, or spreading fear via the conduit of the news media, we perpetuate the horror of existence when we should instead do as Cohle says: "...deny our programming ...stop reproducing...walk hand in hand into extinction, one last midnight..."[7]

"The world is increasingly unthinkable..."[8] So begins Thacker's *In the Dust of This Planet*, and he's right. We are accelerating towards the apocalyptic nadir both as a species and as a culture. If we fail at killing ourselves by changing our climate, then we will surely arrive at a cultural plateau of stunted political and artistic discourses. But this nonhuman turn in the arts and philosophy rejects the exceptionalism of humanity and embraces the uncanny, unthinkable world all around us.

If OOO is the philosophical approach to a "thingified" world, then the work of artist Takeshi Murata shows a truly alien landscape of objects, and what is perhaps most unnerving is the "everyday-ness" of such a landscape. Murata's video for Oneohtrix Point Never's "Problem Areas" is a perfect example, as it portrays a series of CGI objects scattered aimlessly about various mundane locales in a tableau of unsettling normality. Here is the detritus of our everyday lives as consumers, thrown back in our faces as if for the first time. Murata's CGI dips into the uncanny valley, and that is precisely one of the reasons the video is so strange. The familiarity of things – iPhones, VHS tapes, guitars, lemons – has changed. The computer graphics are too clean, but also too fake, to be real.

But Murata's work (as well as Oneohtrix Point Never's) also deals with the Internet and its ability to decontextualize and dehumanize. The Internet is where we can read a news report about a drone strike while watching Japanese pornography, and artists like Murata and OPN foreground this fact as both repulsive and appealing. Visual artist Jon Rafman's video for OPN's "Still Life" plays like a "Worst Hits of the Internet": a furry trapped in quicksand, flashing images of *hentai*, a man wearing girls' panties on his face while holding two guns to each of his temples. In Rafman's video, all things are equal and equally horrifying. But also, every image is shorn of its context, making the experience of watching it somewhat like scrolling through the bottomless pits of Tumblr or Google Images.

The works of Murata, Rafman, and OPN seem to rise from the depths of the Internet in an attempt to show us the dark under-belly of our interconnected existence. Sure, it's shocking, but human beings have always been like this; only now we have the Internet to reveal for ourselves just how shocking.

In addition to OPN, the Sacramento-based musical group Death Grips are known for dredging from the deep web in order to bring the alien things found therein to our surface world.

Like many vaporwave producers, Death Grips take inspiration from the weirder side of the Internet. Their memorable rollout plan for 2012's incredible *NO LOVE DEEP WEB* involved an extensive alternate-reality game (ARG) that used the very fabric of the Internet to promote it. The music videos that accompany their 2013 album *Government Plates* draw from the same uncanny valley as Murata. Ray-traced images of iPods, emojis, statues, and skulls spin against a black background in a way not unlike the objects in "Problem Areas." Paired with the hi-fi frenzy of the music, the videos are a startling experience, giving the impression that the listener is witnessing the weird sights and sounds encountered in the darkest corners of the Internet.

In each of these examples, the human element is absent. In its place are things, both profound and perfunctory. If ever there were an object-oriented aesthetic, these artists would constitute the vanguard, along with vaporwave producers like MACINTOSH PLUS, Infinity Frequencies, and INTERNET CLUB. In addition to being a genre of ghosts, vaporwave is the sound of the outside world of things – electronic technology, mass-produced goods, non-places. And part of this nonhuman aesthetic comes from the visual iconography (more on that later). But in its darkest iterations, vaporwave's other-ness is difficult to pin down. When I started writing this book, I would play my friends the vaporwave songs I enjoyed the most. Thankfully, they were quite patient with me as I bombarded them with questions: "How does this make you *feel?*" "What does this remind you of?" Before I introduced someone to vaporwave for the first time, I attempted to describe its sound and the feelings I associated with it, but I always failed at my attempts. That is, until I actually played a vaporwave song for them, and then they understood. Not everyone reacted the same way, but many of my friends could acknowledge that vaporwave made them feel in ways that were peculiar for a genre of music. They laughed, sometimes grew bored, and often responded with something like, "I've heard this before."

In many ways, vaporwave eluded our explanations, and instead, we found the greatest enjoyment in just listening and delighting in the way the music made us feel. That mixture of dread, nostalgia, and transcendence I feel while listening to something like James Ferraro's *Far Side Virtual* is akin to horrific awe or, to borrow a Lovecraftian term, cosmic horror – a horror of the "outside." The awe and dread described by the characters in H.P. Lovecraft's weird fiction baffle them; they are stunned as their minds struggle to comprehend the alien things before them. They can only describe their own sensations in the presence of great horrors, such as the way the beings smell or what horrible sounds they make. The scientists of Lovecraft's stories usually stumble while trying to describe the terrible shape of the beings – essentially failing at describing what they actually *are*. The opening paragraph of "The Call of Cthulhu" illustrates Lovecraft's knack for summarizing a character's inability to understand the indescribable:

> The most merciful thing in the world, I think, is the inability of the human mind to correlate all its contents. We live on a placid island of ignorance in the midst of black seas of infinity, and it was not meant that we should voyage far. The sciences, each straining in its own direction, have hitherto harmed us little; but some day the piecing together of dissociated knowledge will open up such terrifying vistas of reality, and of our frightful position therein, that we shall either go mad from the revelation or flee from the deadly light into the peace and safety of a new dark age.[9]

Lovecraft's alien gods are truly "unthinkable." They exist at the horizon of thought, and of all the thinkers associated with OOO, Graham Harman draws the sharpest comparison between

Lovecraftian horror and the object-laden universe in which we already live. Dylan Trigg declares that in Harman's writings, he "touches on a fruitful relation between the prosaic and the other-worldly," thereby introducing the truly "alien" into our everyday reality.[10] "The result of this invasion, for Harman," Trigg notes, "is that '[h]umans cease to be masters in their own house'...while phenomenology itself becomes the breeding ground for horror."[11]

Clowns and Killers

Indeed, another breeding ground for this kind of nonhuman horror is the Internet, the vast network that opens up these kinds of "terrifying vistas of reality" for all to see. The Internet is also the place from which much of this thought and art originate. There exist numerous blogs on speculative realism and OOO, and philosophers Timothy Morton and Graham Harman maintain two of the more popular ones. Perhaps no other recent film grapples with the connection between the Internet and cosmic horror better than Drew Goddard and Joss Whedon's *The Cabin in the Woods* (2012). The film can be read in numerous ways: as a critique of the horror film genre, as a comment on the military-industrial complex, and also as a reflection of anthrodecentric thought in the Internet Age. At the film's conclusion, the two remaining characters, Dana and Marty, light up a joint and accept the ultimate destruction of mankind by the Ancient Ones, but this is only after battling the monsters that both serve the purpose of terrorizing the other characters and *subvert* the horror genre at large. In a striking scene, Dana and Marty board an elevator that moves past a multitude of cells, each containing a different monster within. Each monster exists entirely without context; it is as if Dana and Marty were scrolling through images of the menaces. As the camera zooms out, we see a massive menagerie of monsters, many of which are wrenched from the movies that made them famous (the twins from *The Shining*, for instance). It is a visualization of what the Internet does to our history and to the iconic figures of past horror films. During the "system purge" scene in the film, all the monsters are let loose in a stunning display of gruesome terror. The scene exhausts the monsters of their iconographic status: wrenched fully from the contexts of their own movies, they are free to wreak havoc all at once in a new movie.

The Cabin in the Woods essentially samples from the history of horror, but the end result is exhaustive, maximalist even. Goddard and Whedon open the gates and allow all monsters from all time periods free reign. But this is not shameless appropriation. *The Cabin in the Woods* draws a frightening conclusion about our contemporary culture: we are allowed access to everything all the time. All time periods, all settings – everything is up for grabs in the endless archive of the Internet. And *this* is something vaporwave foregrounds well, sometimes in the form of maximalist, hyper-real production (札幌コンテンポラリーby 情報デスクVIRTUAL) and sometimes as VHS-warped hypnagogic pop (*Televised Tragedies* by 18 Carat Affair). Tracks that sample 1980s soft-rock radio hits are listed next to those borrowing from the pristine sounds of twenty-first-century commerce, resulting in a true meltdown of historical boundaries.

But *The Cabin in the Woods* is not *only* scary. The film is hilarious, sometimes in the vein of black comedy, but sometimes its humor is literal, as if the jokes were pulled directly from any contemporary comedy. And there is a mundanity to the humor. Steve Hadley, one of the technicians of the cabin played by Bradley Whitford, teases Mordecai, the "Harbinger" who warns the teens not to go to the cabin, by placing him on speakerphone and laughing at how dedicated Mordecai is to his character as the clichéd messenger foreshadowing death and doom. They then drink and party while the cabin guests are tortured and killed. While the film is cosmically horrifying, it is also comically horrifying, and that mixture of elements is not particular to *The Cabin in the Woods*. Noël Carroll has written on horror and humor as two genres that often blend into one another, whether purposely or by accident. Recounting Freud's theory of the uncanny, Carroll notes, "the road to comic laughter and the road to feelings of uncanniness are unaccountably the same."[12] Carroll's prime figure of horror and humor is the clown, a shapeless being that, by altering certain characteristics, can be hilarious or horrifying (or both):

> [The clown] is a fantastic being, one possessed of an alternate biology, a biology that can withstand blows to the head by hammers and bricks that would be deadly for any mere human, and the clown can sustain falls that would result in serious injury for the rest of us. Not only are clowns exaggeratedly misshapen and, at times, outright travesties of the human form – contortions played on our paradigms of the human shape – they also possess a physical resiliency conjoined with muscular and cognitive disfunctionalities that mark them off as an imaginary species.[13]

This interstitiality exhibited by the clown allows it to shift from a horrific monster to a (sometimes) funny sideshow entertainer. Replace the jolly, goofy smile of a clown with rows of razor-sharp teeth, and suddenly it plays a frequent part in many people's nightmares.

The playfulness of the clown archetype allows it to be interstitial, and vaporwave reflects that sense of playfulness through its typically visible editing and subversive sampling. To me, one of the funniest vaporwave tracks is "drive home thru the stars for you" from esc 不在's stellar album, *black horse*. The song is comprised of a sixteen-second sample repeated four times, and the sample ends right as a pitched-down voice starts to sing, preventing the song from ever moving out of the intro section. The truncated sample subverts our conditioned, entrained ear; we *expect* a pop song to move forward, from section to section, until its conclusion. But what makes "drive home thru the stars for you" funny is that the human voice, the central emotional force in Western popular music, is heard only briefly before the sample repeats again. The vocal line is cut off before it even begins, turning what once was a vocal melody into a burp or a hiccup. Additionally, the sultry electric piano, repeating guitar motif, and easy-listening backbeat (all warped to a slower pitch, emphasizing its forced sensuality) trains us to expect a sexy soft-rock ballad, but instead, the singer cannot properly come in. As soon as the instruments set the stage and a brief pause opens up the space for the vocals, the sample repeats, and we are right back at the beginning. The repeating, poorly spliced samples are funny because they turn the original song into a syrupy mess, exposing the artificiality of soft-rock balladry.

The act of repeating a small audio sample, of jerking it back and forth, and of making it stutter – *abusing* the sample at hand – can be quite comical to hear, as in "花の専門店" by MACINTOSH PLUS or "R × S = {(r1, r2, ..., rn, s1, s2, ..., sm) | (r1, r2, ..., rn) ∈ R, (s1, s2, ..., sm) ∈ S}" by Transilvanian Hunger. In both cases, the sample abuse makes the songs feel extremely shaky, as if they are about to topple and fall apart under the hand of the producer, but it is the latter example that, along with the rest of the Transilvanian Hunger album on which it is included, successfully showcases vaporwave's comedic side. Entitled 葛城 ミサト (2013) (which roughly translates to "Misato Katsuragi," a character from the critically acclaimed anime *Neon Genesis Evangelion*), the album features chopped and screwed soft-rock hits as well as some of the strangest song titles of any vaporwave release, such as "a = Δv = v – v0 Δt Δt," "01110100 01101000 01100101 0100000 01100101 01101110 01100100," and "G1, G2, ..., Gm g f1(A1'), f2(A2'), ..., fk(Ak') (r)." When paired with the deformed samples of adult contemporary music, these mathematical titles appear entirely out of place, but that is the point. Transilvanian Hunger is attempting to deface these sultry songs at all costs by slowing them down to a nauseating slur, chopping them into hiccups and moans, and giving them ridiculous song names that are the furthest thing from a typical pop title.

The tracks on 葛城 ミサト remind me of Martin Arnold's *Passage à l'acte* (1993), an experimental film composed entirely from a scene in *To Kill a Mockingbird* (1962) during which Atticus Finch eats breakfast with his children, Scout and Jem. Arnold repeats tiny segments of the film clip over and over, gradually progressing through the entire scene itself. Watching the characters of such a beloved film jerk back and forth while others in the frame wear banal or bored facial expressions is quite disturbing. Arnold emphasizes the briefest moments in the film and then repeats them until they *become* the film we are watching. Ultimately, by manipulating these in-between moments in an otherwise short and forgettable scene, Arnold uncovers hidden tension between the characters in the film. The scene becomes a surreal reworking of a miserable family meal or perhaps a glimpse into the life of Atticus Finch and his family when the cameras are turned off. What is important to note is that, at times, *Passage à l'acte* is funny. There is a darkly comedic moment as Arnold violently manipulates the film while Scout responds to her brother with, "I'm trying!" As the film skips and she stutters to spit the line out, the sounds she makes are twangy and bizarre, but funny nonetheless.

Arnold made *Passage à l'acte* fifteen to twenty years before the popularity of YouTube Poop (YTP), a video remix genre born from and still thriving on YouTube, but both Arnold's film and the slew of YTPs that can be found on the Internet scan as both comic and disquieting. Ethnographer and YouTube scholar Michael Wesch describes YTP as "absurdist remixes that ape and mock the lowest technical and aesthetic standards of remix culture to comment on remix culture itself."[14] This is an apt description of a crude, often humorous, and sometimes annoying genre of video remixing that draws source material from television shows such as *Spongebob Squarepants*, *King of the Hill*, *Saved by the Bell*, and even infomercials such as those popularized by television salesperson Billy Mays.

To turn a video into a "poop" of itself, one has to do something very similar to what Martin Arnold did to the breakfast scene in *To Kill a Mockingbird* and what a producer like Transilvanian Hunger does to radio pop. The hilarious YTP known as "Hank of the Hill," uploaded to YouTube by DurhamrockerZ, tweaks the original episode of *King of the Hill* in several hilarious ways. The video opens with a rushed title sequence directly after Hank Hill iconically pops the tab on his beer. Then Hank, Bill, and Dale watch a television advertisement for a lawn-mowing expo narrated by an overzealous announcer, but the entire video skips in a frenetic fashion, which makes the announcer repeat a certain phrase again and again until it sounds like "Seaking," a popular Pokémon character. At this point, an image of the Seaking character flashes on the screen, and we are not even forty seconds into the video. But, like *Passage à l'acte*, "Hank of the Hill" and other YTPs draw attention to the darker, peripheral moments of transition that go unnoticed by the casual viewer. Around two minutes into "Hank of the Hill," Peggy informs Hank he will have to go to Dallas with her if he wants to be her Boggle coach, at which point Hank responds incredulously with, "Dallas?" Hank's voice is then reversed to sound like "Salad?" followed by a slow close-up of his face in transition from looking at Peggy to looking elsewhere. The music is suddenly ominous, and the expression on Hank's face is one of slight disgust, subdued anger, and drunken stupidity. By lingering menacingly on Hank's strange and uncharacteristic facial expression, DurhamrockerZ creates new meaning out of the brief moments in-between surface-level dialogue and plot-advancing action in the show. This new meaning (a combination of unease, slight tension, and foreboding) can only be found and accentuated in the hidden gaps we either ignore or do not notice when watching a typical episode of *King of the Hill*.

Transilvanian Hunger and the more talented YTP producers like DurhamrockerZ are the descendants of experimenters like Martin Arnold as well as culture jammers such as the 1970s Bay Area band Negativland and pop-culture obliterator John Oswald. Though Oswald and Negativland are more of the prankster variety of experimental artists, their approach to plunderphonics involves severely deforming an original recording until it becomes something else. Usually the source material is a pop mega-hit, such as U2's "I Still Haven't Found What I'm Looking For," which is parodied on Negativland's EP entitled *U2*. Or, Michael Jackson's "Bad," which is shredded and warped into a stuttering mess by John Oswald on "Dab." For both of these subversive artists, effacing the most popular and commercial forms of music exposes pop culture as a fraud, an industry designed to sell good feelings and reinforce the status quo. By throwing a song like "Bad" on the chopping block and remixing it lengthily in a sampler, Oswald reveals the hidden worlds beneath the sterile glow of commercially successful music (which is also exemplified by the samples of radio personality Casey Kasem losing his cool and cussing throughout the *U2* EP).

But these composers do not only parody the zeitgeist – they also trash the past. Take *The Cabin in the Woods* – the film is as much an homage to the horror genre as an elaborate game played with the iconic figures of horror-film history. Like any good piece of postmodern art, *Cabin* walks the line between homage and parody but ultimately arrives at an unambiguous conclusion: destroy all history. *Cabin* implies everything should go to make way for a clean slate and a chance to start again new.

This sentiment is obviously self-destructive, but the aesthetic decision to destroy a work of art from the inside out (including all humans along with it) has been utilized in other films in the 2010s, including Lars von Trier's end-of-the-world tale, *Melancholia* (2011), as well as the Adult Swim viral hit *Too Many Cooks* (2014).

A short "infomercial" that aired on Adult Swim early one late-October morning, writer-director Casper Kelly's *Too Many Cooks* is a surreal and violent parody of a cutesy 90s-style family sitcom that struggles to move past the title sequence, frequently morphs into various other television genres, and culminates in the majority of the characters either trapped in their roles forever or murdered by an omnipresent killer. The short became a viral hit. The creators were interviewed; articles analyzed the film's appeal; and even CNN offered up their own 2016 Presidential Election parody of the short.[15] For about a week in early November, you could not surf anywhere on the Internet without encountering the viral hit of a fake sitcom continually undermining itself and falling apart.

Why did this disturbing and comical video – a mere programming blip aired while the majority of Americans were fast asleep – strike such a nerve? First, like *The Cabin in the Woods*, *Too Many Cooks* plays with our knowledge of pop-culture history while also reminding us of the chintzy television sitcoms we grew up with, the wildly popular ones that portrayed family life as unrealistically as Epcot portrays a handful of the world's countries. Shows like *The Brady Bunch*, *Alf*, and *Full House* presented American viewers of the 1970s, 80s, and 90s with a half-hour of perfect, white, heteronormative families, while their daytime counterparts, soap operas, typically offered the dramatic struggles of affluent, privileged families. Though several soap operas are still programmed today on cable television, many of the aforementioned family sitcoms can only be seen now as reruns or streamed online, and their simplistic presentation of the modern family dynamic has not aged well. But *Too Many Cooks* does not just parody family sitcoms and soaps. Instead, all of television history is surveyed in the film, and the simplest, most emotionally one-dimensional genres and tropes are mocked: the clean police procedural, the Saturday-morning action cartoon, and even the space opera. Casper Kelly and his team portray what happens when the diegeses of these television shows become so self-aware that they abort themselves, first through exhaustive repetition and then by the machete of a sinister murderer.

What vaporwave does to pop music, *Too Many Cooks* does to pre-millennial/pre-Internet Age television. The nauseatingly hooky "Too Many Cooks" musical theme subverts the typical TV theme by looping for nearly the entire length of the short film and repeatedly introducing new families and characters, including anthropomorphic Alf-like characters such as Smarf, "Pie," and "Coat." There is even a sequence that mimics the soap opera *Falcon Crest*, but the introduction and opening theme loop like a skipping record.

Throughout the first half of the short, during which the repeated sections become slowly more surreal, a seedy character can be seen lurking in the background. That character then breaks fully into the diegesis only to murder and eat most of the cast. In a shocking scene, the murderer chases a young girl named Katie Adkins off the pristine set of her sitcom and through the grungy alleys of the backlot, her shining "Katie Adkins" name credit from the title sequence following her. He then finds her by the glow of her name tag, and as she desperately tries to hide the light, the killer slashes her.

At this point, *Too Many Cooks* has subverted itself entirely, destroying the very parody it sets up for us at the beginning (a sitcom that gets stuck in the title sequence and exhaustively keeps introducing new characters and tropes). Now, the short is a sitcom with some outside killer introduced to dismantle the established universe of the TV show. In one way, the murderer is our contemporary culture traveling back into the past to trash it entirely. He is the digital technology of our time allegorized and let loose in the warm glow of television's analog domain, a virus swimming through a complex and unsuspecting system. This system is our history, which has been blown apart by the Internet's promise of allowing, as Radiohead reminds us, "everything all of the time."[16] The killer is not waging war on past forms and styles but instead stalking and slaying the television icons of our pop-cultural history, and his bloodthirsty destruction reminds us that we can never truly go back to the pre-9/11, pre-Internet culture that brought us *Full House* and *Family Matters*. It is worth noting that the murderer in *Too Many Cooks* is obviously styled after Jack Torrance in Stanley Kubrick's *The Shining* (1980). Jack, the struggling alcoholic and frustrated father in Kubrick's masterpiece, is a unique character in horror-film history in that he has existed before and will presumably exist again in the world of the film. He is a disabler of history, an anachronism who wanders in and out of time and who threatens the established familial order by attempting to murder his wife and son. Like Jack, the murderer in *Too Many Cooks* is always present – peeking behind a corner or looming in the background – until he arrives and finishes the job of dismantling the neat order of the sitcoms in which he roams.

At the end, all the characters from *Too Many Cooks* are placed in their respective blue cells in the style of *The Brady Bunch*'s title sequence, but the matrix is more massive than the three-by-three grid of the Brady's and not unlike the monstrous menagerie in *The Cabin in the Woods*. The immense grid with all the characters represents the final resting place of our history – the Internet, a great decontextualizing platform where all things can be surveyed and saved in the Cloud.

Chapter 3

Lost Futures and Consumer Dreams: Hauntology and the Sounds of Capital

All of this has happened before, and it will all happen again.
– *from* Peter Pan *(1953)¹*

All that is solid melts into PR.
– *Mark Fisher²*

By the first decade of the twenty-first century, the crisis of historicity in contemporary art had reached a watershed moment. Both popular and experimental musicians mined the immediate and the far-reaching pasts to compose music reminiscent of bygone eras. Film and television classics, such as *Miami Vice* and John Carpenter's *Halloween* franchise, were revived as remakes, and pop music began its decade-long-and-counting worship of the American 1980s. It seemed that as culture moved forward into the early 2010s, visual art, film, and music regressed further into the analog past – a move fulfilling theorist Fredric Jameson's lament that "stylistic innovation is no longer possible."³ This haunting of the present culture by the past has often been associated with "hauntology," a term first introduced by Jacques Derrida in his prophetic critique of global capitalism, *Specters of Marx: The State of the Debt, the Work of Mourning & the New International*. Writing in the early 1990s, Derrida challenged historian Francis Fukuyama's concept that with the fall of the Berlin Wall, the world is now living at the "end of history" and that global capitalism will forever reign supreme. Hauntology has now widened to include the multiple art movements that magnify the crisis of historicity so prevalently theorized in particular by Jameson and cultural theorist Linda Hutcheon in their respective analyses of postmodernism and, in particular, postmodern film and music. Hauntology is a political and aesthetic update to their theories of nostalgia and history in postmodern art and furthers Derrida's claim that the "future can only be for ghosts. And the past."[4]

To understand how we arrived at a haunted culture, we must survey the most prevalent cultural mode of the past thirty years – postmodernism – and chart its evolution. Linda Hutcheon and Fredric Jameson, two of the most profound cultural critics in recent history, propose distinct critiques of postmodernism, each grappling with the roles of pastiche and politics in order to arrive at separate theories of history in postmodern art. Hutcheon analyzes Jameson's theory of postmodern pastiche, or the "mimicry of other styles,"[5] by maintaining that it is anything but what Jameson calls "blank parody."[6] That is, Hutcheon acknowledges the political bite of parody and counters Jameson's idea that postmodern pastiche lacks the humor of parody and is "without parody's ulterior motive."[7] For Hutcheon, postmodernism is "more willfully compromised, more ideologically ambivalent or contradictory" and "exploits and subverts that which went before."[8] Postmodernism can then be considered a political artistic practice or mode because it undermines the assumptions about art, language, and culture that spectators hold. It challenges art by deconstructing everything that came before while still remaining self-reflexive. These characteristics are chief in understanding these theorists' differing opinions of postmodernism and its relation to history.

One of the primary notions upheld by both Hutcheon and Jameson is that history is unknowable, yet they both offer suggestions as to how we interact with such unknowability. Hutcheon and Jameson turn to film to tackle our perception of history as film both presents and complicates historical "reality." Hutcheon asserts that "[postmodern films] suggest...there

31

is no directly and naturally accessible past 'real' for us today: we can only know – and construct – the past through its traces, its representations."[9] Like other forms of postmodern art, postmodern films are heavily intertextual and stress the unknowability of the past. Jameson accentuates the imagery of the past in these films (what he terms "nostalgia films") as "[seeking] to reawaken a sense of the past associated with those [art objects]."[10] His example is *Star Wars*, a film that manipulates the images of certain bygone media – the serial adventure, in particular – to create a form of nostalgic art. These "nostalgia films" give the impression of the past through "pop images and stereotypes about the past" because history itself is of course unknowable.[11] Nostalgia is commodified via the reevaluation and championing of stereotypes and is injected into films both Jameson and Hutcheon deem as "postmodern." It is no surprise then that *Star Wars*, with its numerous references to the pop-serial format, was lauded by those moviegoers who grew up watching afternoon adventure stories a couple of decades before its release.

Though they disagree over postmodernism as a political mode, James and Hutcheon both acknowledge that it is in some way a symptom of capitalism. Hutcheon's model of postmodernism emphasizes capitalism's role as an aid to postmodern artists in their critique of the culture industry. For Hutcheon, postmodernism "exploits its 'insider' position in order to begin a subversion from within, to talk to consumers in a capitalist society in a way that will get us where we live, so to speak."[12] Postmodernism calls attention to the reality that in the age of commodified culture, art has to be produced within the capitalist market; therefore, culture and industry always intertwine. However, Hutcheon contends that postmodern art undermines the capitalist market by critiquing the very system in which it is created and distributed to the masses. Again, Hutcheon does not separate politics from postmodernism, a point seen most clearly in her definition of postmodern parody.

Jameson agrees to a point here. He categorizes postmodernism as such:

> [Postmodernism] is...a periodizing concept whose function is to correlate the emergence of new formal features in culture with the emergence of a new type of social life and a new economic order – what is often euphemistically called modernization, post-industrial or consumer society, the society of the media or the spectacle, or multinational capitalism.[13]

Though Jameson does not explicitly state that postmodernism is politically subversive in the manner Hutcheon outlines, he does note its place in history. With the realization of global capitalism, postmodern art pulls from various times and places to create a pastiche that reflects the commodification of culture without necessarily critiquing it openly. Rampant consumerism allows artists to willfully mix media to create a new form of artistic appropriation that erases time and space, a move that foreshadows the hauntology of the twenty-first century. These various forms of postmodern art, according to Jameson, complicate our relationship to history by turning it into a commodity.

Ultimately, the commodification of the past and its stereotypes is still a product of the capitalist market, and these postmodern films reflect such a relationship to capitalism. Hutcheon maintains that postmodernism "wants to use [its] 'insider' position to 'de-doxify' the 'givens' that 'go without saying' in those grand systems" – patriarchy and capitalism, namely.[14] Again, Hutcheon writes of the subversive qualities of postmodernism, which challenge the *doxa* put in place by these grand systems. The result is a critique of capitalism and patriarchy by way of insider subversion, but for Jameson, this insider position is a cause for concern. He calls these postmodern films "a terrible indictment of consumer capitalism itself" and "an alarming and pathological symptom of a society that has become incapable of dealing with time and history."[15] He does not concern himself with postmodernism's supposed propensity to undermine the grand systems in order to preclude them from continuing. Instead, he diagnoses our supposed popularizing of the past and its stereotypes as a malignancy of capitalism. History, for Jameson, now belongs in an "imaginary museum" in which all the art objects of the past can be appropriated for monetary gain, and his jeremiad concludes with his prediction of "the imprisonment of the past."[16] His critique of postmodernism's obsession with history is more a fearful assertion of art's failure than Hutcheon's, and though their theories wrestle with art's placement in capitalism after the middle of the twentieth century, they are challenged by the turn of the twenty-first century by the next historical crisis occurring with the dawn of a new era in capitalism.

The spread of global capitalism comes with an increased crisis of historicity in art. Jameson mentions the "new moment of capitalism" as a period ranging "from the post-war boom in the United States in the late 1940s and early 1950s or, in France, from the establishment of the Fifth Republic in 1958."[17] From this "new moment of capitalism" come the postmodern artists who produce art that is highly self-reflexive and subversive in a capitalist market. Whether they are categorically defined as Jameson's pastiche or Hutcheon's parody, they challenge artistic norms and complicate the past and our relation to it.

For Jacques Derrida, however, the next turning point occurs with the fall of the Berlin Wall, ushering in the "end of history" and sparking a new era of global capitalism. A grand critique of neoliberalism's victory with the collapse of the Berlin Wall is at the heart of Derrida's *Specters of Marx*, in which he first coins "hauntology" as that which "begins by coming back."[18] For Derrida, the specter is the spirit of Marxism returning and "haunting" as "some 'thing' that remains difficult to name: neither soul nor body, and both one and the other."[19] We can consider hauntology as the past's idealized portrait of a brave, new future haunting the present and also as an update to postmodernism's critique of history.

This shift in focus from mining the cultural past for pastiche or parody to mourning a lost future differentiates postmodernism from hauntology. Whereas postmodernism toys with history via an increased skepticism in truly "knowing" the past, hauntology posits that the past notions of the future have in some way failed, causing a disruption of time as an orderly sequence of past, present, and future. Much of this discussion of the future's failure stems from Derrida's blistering critique of liberal democracy's triumph after the fall of the Berlin Wall. His indictment of such belief comes midway through *Specters of Marx*:

Instead of singing the advent of the ideal of liberal democracy and of the capitalist market in the euphoria of the end of history, instead of celebrating the "end of ideologies" and the end of the great emancipatory discourses, let us never neglect this obvious macroscopic fact...no degree of progress allows one to ignore that never before...have so many men, women, and children been subjugated, starved, or exterminated on the earth.[20]

For Derrida, no celebration must be had with regards to global capitalism, for it does not spell redemption from political or personal suffering. He illustrates that such belief in the power of capitalism as a freeing institution is foolish, for it will not promise utopia. With more suffering mounting every day in the wake of the newest moment of capitalism, Derrida argues we are nowhere near the "end of history." Hauntology, therefore, is the artistic mode of realizing this failure of the future that was promised in the past. It is the dismantling of the definitions of past, present, and future and is absolutely political in its critique of capitalism. Hauntology then is unlike Jameson's pastiche in that it complicates the past (specifically, the past's image of the future) in order to call attention to capitalism's destructive nature as a subjugating force that only fools others into thinking it can eradicate "history" – i.e. the ideologies Derrida mentions above.

Thus, hauntological art serves as a political and aesthetic update to Jameson's and Hutcheon's theories of postmodernism by erasing any sense of time or space in art and by illustrating the past's continual reminder of the future's failure in the form of haunting. This haunting always implies some kind of distance between the specter and that which is haunted (the present). Theorist Mark Fisher's primary example of this distant spooky action is *The Shining*. The characters and the setting of *The Shining* are hauntological in that they challenge politics and history after the supposed "end of history." For example, Jack Torrance, played by Jack Nicholson, is the caretaker of the Overlook Hotel and does not exist in linear time in the film. Fisher furthers Jack's position as timeless:

> Jack is one who takes care, but also one who lacks any agency of his own. Insofar as he belongs to the hotel, he exists only in a caretaker capacity, as one who merely insures that the past (the obscene, homicidal underside of patriarchy) will keep repeating.[21]

Jack Torrance is the harbinger of hauntology in that he embodies Derrida's claim that the past will continue to haunt and has continued to haunt the present since its initial haunting. He is the eternal return of history acting at the distance afforded him by his existence outside time. Ultimately Jack is the antithesis to Jameson's "imprisonment of the past" as one of postmodernism's defining characteristics. Whereas postmodernism captures and appropriates the past, hauntology sets the past free to disestablish time as a sequence and transform it into a looping construction. This form of repeating time in *The Shining* also combats Hutcheon's idea of postmodernism as a challenge to certain grand systems of narrative. Hauntological art brings to light the reality that these grand systems will always continue because the past will always repeat. At the end of *The Shining*, the picture of a grinning Jack Torrance from the 1920s indicates his position outside time and suggests his role as the spirit of evil, which is always returning. Fisher also associates the horror of Jack's timelessness with atemporality and further remarks on the eeriness of the film's setting, deeming it "a kind of architecture of anachronism" in which "one door can lead into a ballroom endlessly playing dreamy delirious 1920s pop, and another can reveal a moldering corpse, whose corridors extend in time as well as space."[22] The Overlook Hotel is the locus of haunting in which various pieces of the past intermix with the present to create an anachronism of time and space. If Jameson's "imaginary museum" could serve as the model for postmodernism, then the Overlook Hotel is the hauntological arena in which time as a repeating construct is acted out. Whereas former artistic styles and conventions are appropriated and critiqued in the "imaginary museum," history itself repeats until time and space disintegrate in the Overlook, and as the caretaker, Jack Torrance is the one who carries out the disintegration.

And the music playing in the Overlook, the dreamy ballroom music and the eerie rendition of "Midnight, the Stars and You," helps create an atmosphere of atemporality. The first time we hear the Overlook's music is when Jack transports back into the 1920s to attend a soirée with the other guests of that time period, and of course there is the famous end scene as we see that Jack has literally always been the caretaker, his devilish grin haunting us from the American 1920s while the faint sounds of Al Bowlly drift in the background. The ballroom music sets the foreboding mood of the Overlook, and it also reminds viewers that the Overlook stands outside time.

As a nod to this film, experimental artist James Leyland Kirby named one of his many musical projects The Caretaker after Jack's occupation in the film, and his creative process fittingly involves warping and looping vinyl clips of ballroom music that evoke the classical Hollywood era of the thirties and forties – as well as the haunting music heard in *The Shining*. The genre of music popularized by The Caretaker and other composers (such as those on the Ghost Box record label) has been termed "hauntology" by music critics because it is meant to evoke a feeling of the past haunting the present. Hauntological music calls attention to the looping structure of history and the eeriness of temporal breakdown. The Caretaker's 1999 album *Selected Memories from the Haunted Ballroom*, in particular, pays homage to *The Shining* and is the hauntology genre in its most distilled form. These are the tunes heard while drifting through the Overlook, wandering in and out of grand hallways, lost in time. The album is not an intertextual pastiche meant to pull from all areas of history but is instead a remarkably precise album in its evocations. It is an album of music that *sounds* like the past returning to haunt the present. His 2011 album, *An Empty Bliss Beyond this World*, takes his hauntological music a step further. With song titles like "All you are going to want to do is get back there" and "I feel as if I might be vanishing," the album is the sound of deep nostalgia, a loss of something great and far removed from our time. By cutting his samples into short, jagged loops and applying heavy distortion, reverb, and vinyl decay, The Caretaker manipulates our perceived stereotypes of the past as sounding old and worn out. We long for a time evoked by The Caretaker – a time of distant ballroom music on warped analog media – that no longer exists and perhaps never existed at all. The Caretaker's music implies a sense of timelessness, which is fitting for a musical project named after Jack Torrance's eternal position of power in the Overlook.

In addition to dismantling a sense of time, hauntological art breaks down spatial continuity as well. Mark Fisher draws on anthropologist Marc Augé's idea of the "non-place" as a product of capitalism and a prime site of spatial disintegration. Such "non-places" are "airports, retail parks, and chain stores which resemble one another more than they resemble the particular spaces in which they are located."[23] These locations are signifiers of capitalist consumption in that they serve only to promote the buying and selling of goods. They can be found in multiple places in multiple cities, thus dissolving a sense of place belonging to any one location. Like the Overlook, these areas of consumption seem to lack any spatial tangibility. They are as unreal in nature as Kubrick's menacing and enigmatic hotel. Art and commerce fuse almost entirely in these "non-places" as rampant consumerism reaches a new peak in the era of global capitalism. A consumer wandering through a typical "nonplace," like a mall for example, should take note of the sounds as well as the images of such a drained structure. It is no coincidence that the shopping mall is a symbol used by multiple vaporwave composers to evoke a place in which their warped music could be heard.

Vaporwave is the music of "non-times" and "non-places" because it is skeptical of what consumer culture has done to time and space. The bulk of vaporwave is critical of late capitalism at every stage of its production, from its source material to the way the music is distributed and sold (if at all). As I have stated before, an over-arching definition of vaporwave is harmful, for something so compartmentalizing as a "How-To Guide" for making vaporwave or a one-sentence summation of the genre seems out of step with the anti-corporatism of the vaporwave composers. But identifying the multiple characteristics of vaporwave that critique consumerism and the culture industry can illustrate the political power of this microgenre.

Peripheral Music

First, the source material of many vaporwave compositions is typically some form of peripheral or incidental music – that is, music designed for playback at the peripheries of our daily life, rarely intended for direct listening. Vaporwave producers sample the music we encounter in airports, supermarkets, waiting rooms, shopping malls, and elevators, as well as the music we hear when we are placed on hold during a routine phone call or during a commercial while waiting for a television program to resume. This is music we hear as we perform a perfunctory, boring, but necessary action that typically involves consumption, and the music's purpose is to turn our mind-numbing experience into something a bit less vapid while trying to sell us something in the process. It is the lubricant that glides us along our journey of daily material existence, from non-place to non-place, engaging in the glories of the free market while narcotizing ourselves to discomfort. This unobtrusive music can take many forms: Muzak, easy-listening, middle-of-the-road radio (MOR), smooth jazz, glitzy New Age, television bumpers, or other forms of anodyne music that populate our consumerist experience.

Muzak has long held a utilitarian function in Western modern life, from filling the empty space of a corporate office to irking us as we sit in a physician's waiting room. Joseph Lanza's paean to piped music, *Elevator Music: A Surreal History of Muzak, Easy-Listening, and Other Moodsong*, details the history of Muzak's rise from a musical pick-me-up meant to guide the work force happily through the day to the oft-maligned anesthetic regarded as such by many today. Lanza's own succinct definition of Muzak is "music made and programmed for business environments to reduce stress, combat fatigue, and enhance sales," and this is a fairly standard definition for the incidental music made by the Muzak® company itself.[24] But perhaps Queens College Professor Gary Gumpert offers a better definition of Muzak:

Muzak is music that is put in a Laundromat. It's been bathed; and all of its passion gotten rid of. It's there; it doesn't make a wave. It's just a kind of amniotic fluid that surrounds us; and it never startles us, it is never too loud, it is never too silent; it's always there...[25]

Gumpert is drawn to the near-invisibility of Muzak by alerting us to its universality. It is always around us in some way, whether we are watching television, staring at a DVD menu screen, or shopping for clothes. Muzak is intended to be just another part of our environment, something composer Erik Satie sought to accomplish with his "furniture music," but often presents itself as the obvious corporate solution to the modern dread that accompanies unpleasant excursions into the modern world.[26] These "tenuous moments," as Lanza calls them, can include "a pivotal office engagement, another stay of execution in the dentist's waiting room, or the nail-biting anticipation of a late plane arrival."[27] This is not the music we serenade a guest with or that we analyze in order to discover its most elemental qualities, but vaporwave dissolves this notion. Vaporwave recontextualizes elevator music by sampling snippets from the most prosaic musical rubbish and presenting them in a different way, forcing us to reconsider Muzak's subversive qualities and its inane catchiness – to intently *listen* to the music that has been humming just outside our perception for decades. Vaporwave engages in an act of reframing, not necessarily to parody the ceaseless soft rock of shopping malls or the mood music of waiting rooms (though, as we've seen, some vaporwave can be both humorous and unsettling), but instead to remind listeners of its omnipresence and, therefore, to wake us up to the corporatist society in which we are trapped.

Vaporwave takes the fit, smiling, white-teethed mask off Muzak and replaces it with a more sinister face – the dead stare of unfettered capitalism. This switcheroo reminds us of Muzak's history with capitalism's incessant push to keep the populace working, no matter the mental condition, physical disability, or personal circumstance. Lanza details the musical experiments performed at the U.S. Army Human Engineering Laboratories involving piped music and soldiers' vigilance during long stretches of tedium, as well as Muzak's role in calming cattle as they "[go] to the hereafter" in some early-1970s Illinois slaughter-houses.[28] Vaporwave's reframing of Muzak shows us these moments in the history of capitalism – not the chipper office clerk gleefully performing daily duties to the ditties of soft-rock FM radio but the sounds of Kenny G playing to panicked cattle on a conveyor belt.

Lanza's book concludes with the naïve allegation that Muzak is "a distillation of the happiness that modern technology has promised."[29] The ending statement may come as no surprise considering the majority of Lanza's history of Muzak is viewed through rose-colored lenses, but it is still a problematic conclusion to a book about corporate music designed to keep us shopping and soothe us as we have our cavities filled. An album like the aforementioned *Chuck Person's Eccojams Vol. 1* provides a more startling and accurate critique of mood music and our relation to it. Lopatin distorts, warps, loops, and destroys samples of radio hits such as Fleetwood Mac's "Gypsy" on the propulsive track "Eccojam B2." "B2" ends with a looped sample of "Gypsy" slowed to a drawling plod that never gets to the hook of the song ("Lightning strikes maybe once, maybe twice / Oh, and it lights up the night / And you see your – / Lightning strikes…" and so forth), but the first half of the song is a noisy and distorted sample of a pop song that is continually self-destructing. It is a horrifying listen, especially as it skips and the clicking of the sample begins to sound like a clock ticking away the seconds as the song morphs. "B2" is the sound of your worst experience in a public "non-place," as the FM radio plays, the clock ticks, and the world around melts before your very eyes. Then suddenly, the pain ceases and the soothing, warped sounds of "Gypsy" carry you away to oblivion.

Sensory Experience

Second, the vaporwave aesthetic relies heavily on certain images that evoke life under capitalism, both past and present. In particular, vaporwave album covers draw heavily from images of commerce, metropolises, computers, televisions, and numerous other "non-places" and technological media. In this way, these covers usually establish a setting or mood of the album, which arguably serves the same purpose for any other album cover in any other genre of music, but for vaporwave, the album cover is typically explicit in its representation and in thematically furthering the album overall. As Dylan Trigg reminds us, a place can immediately transport us to another time period, perhaps one we never experienced but know well from visual culture, and this form of time travel is usually set off by encountering the imagery of a specific place. For example, the album cover for CULTURE ISLAND by vaporwave producer Miami Vice is a washed out, hazy photograph of palm trees against a setting sun. I have unfortunately never been to Miami, but I have been to many beaches and have seen pictures and videos of Miami in my lifetime. Regardless, the album cover, with its faded appearance, immediately places me on a beach during sundown in some far-distant time period, a time before digital cameras and enhanced resolution. When I listen to the album while looking at this album cover, the effect is multisensory – I am recalling a sunny trip to Miami that I never took.

Or take, for example, the album cover for Topographic Maps'
Tropical Disturbances: a heavily colorized photograph of a pool
party set in the 1980s perhaps. Listening to the album and staring
at the album cover transports me to a warm, exotic locale set in
a time before my own. Both image and music combine to create
that album's particular, sometimes unique aesthetic. Perhaps this
stems from a push by Internet composers to splinter genres into
infinitely smaller and smaller subgenres. After all, casinowave,
an offshoot of vaporwave, utilizes the sights and sounds of
being in a casino, while VHS-wave places the listener in a time
of analog televisions. Genre tags notwithstanding, vaporwave
albums work best when consumed as a total sensory experience.
Even the song titles usually play a part in building a particular
album's aesthetic. Look at some of the track titles for *Tropical
Disturbances* ("Golden Daze," "Seabreeze," "Rum Runner") or
18 Carat Affair's analog technology sampler *Televised Tragedies*
("Fall Catalog," "Home Box Office," "Tonights Low").

The average vaporwave album is incredibly cohesive, with
all artistic elements of a release working towards some unifying
theme particular to that album, but what is common among
most vaporwave albums is that they are "set" in the times and
places of Western capitalistic society. Whether they are requiems
for early capitalism or glaring reflections of our own moment
in late capitalism, the majority of vaporwave albums can be
read as indictments of life under the sign of consumption. In
an especially influential and controversial article for *Dummy*,
musicologist Adam Harper provocatively sums up vaporwave's
possible subversive elements while accurately pinpointing the
metaphorical setting wherein these warped sounds of commerce
play out:

Today and tomorrow, capital lives everywhere, in our TVs,
phones and minds, but nowhere is it more holy than in
the gleaming temples of its interface with the public – the

office lobby, the hotel reception area, and most of all, the shopping mall. This music belongs in the *plaza*, literal and metaphorical, real and imaginary – the public space that is the nexus of infinite social, cultural and financial transactions and the scene of their greatest activity and spectacle.[30]

The virtual plaza is a proper setting for the sounds of vaporwave, and Harper reminds us that the polytendriled entity of capital is all around us. Harper posits that artists like New Dreams Ltd and INTERNET CLUB create anti-capitalist music that metaphorizes the vaporization of all things under late capitalism, and the virtual plaza is the structure comprised of all the gleaming towers of commerce built upon the code-destroying nexus of capital. It is the ultimate "non-place" – a place not unlike the Overlook in which we drift and consume, lulled by the saccharine tones of Muzak.

Vaporpunk

But, for the most part, there is a product we cannot consume in the virtual plaza, and that is vaporwave itself. Vaporwave is the sound of the virtual plaza reframed and thrown back at us in an attempt to reveal for us capital's stronghold on our existence, but its method of production and distribution lies totally outside the financial transactions that occur in the plaza. Vaporwave was born on the Internet and is largely offered for free online via individual artists' Bandcamp pages and other file-sharing sites. No showy press photos, no extensive PR campaigns, no advertising, little mainstream critical recognition – vaporwave may be the first "post-music-scene" genre. This obscurity is reasonably part of the genre's appeal. Stumbling onto vaporwave for the first time, I felt I was happening upon an entire microcosm of artists operating prolifically right under my nose. With the exception of Saint Pepsi, the vaporwave-turned-future-funk project of Ryan DeRobertis (who now produces music under the name Skylar Spence), no other vaporwave producer has risen to even a level of "indie" fame, let alone mainstream acceptance. There are no big-budget vaporwave productions, and until the day that happens (if it ever does), vaporwave producers will remain below the popular radar, churning out music for little to no profit, and constantly growing with each new guerilla release.

An example of this kind of underground, DIY aesthetic is SPF420, the online music-venue-meets-hangout that served as the birthplace of vaporwave and where the vaporwave all-stars got their respective starts. After becoming disenchanted with her local noise scene, the co-founder of SPF420 turned to the online music infosphere and found "a group of people who were just as interested in music that was not in their area," mainly on the massive music database Last.fm.[31] After hosting proto-SPF420 TinyChat shows, she and the community she helped establish migrated to Turntable.fm to discuss favorite bands and put on shows, and from there, SPF420 was formed. "We started SPF420 because we loved music of all kinds, and most importantly, we loved the people that were supporters of listening to all styles of music," she says. "Nothing was 'bad' to us, except being a negative person and not being open. We created a community... everyone wants to have a sense of community."[32]

That sense of welcoming community allowed artists like Portland, OR-based producer and visual artist Ramona Xavier to find other like-minded lovers of music and to develop her sound as one of the preeminent producers of her time. "I literally didn't know anybody [in real life] until 2012, when I ran away and moved to Portland," says Xavier, after which she met the soon-to-be co-founders of SPF420 and together helped to create the vaporwave genre.[33] Vaporwave is as much a community as it is a genre and has its roots in the DIY attitude. In this way, vaporwave has become something like the "new punk" or the "Internet punk" – coming from the online underground yet growing with an emphasis on welcoming others. The formation of the genre was a grassroots approach that shows musical history can still occur without the industrial tentacles of the music-business-at-large constricting every stage of artistic creation in the name of the dollar.

Finally, perhaps vaporwave's ultimate defacement of the culture industry is the lack of transparency between artist moniker and producer. As mentioned before, in the case of Ramona Xavier, there are several monikers that can be traced to her name. This sort of prolific anonymity allows a burgeoning community to appear much more expansive than it is and to also cement the specific traits of a genre early in its development. Xavier's projects are often cited as premier examples of the vaporwave genre, with MACINTOSH PLUS usually cited as the alias that introduced vaporwave to a wider demographic.

No other vaporwave release has received such acclaim, exposure, or vitriol as MACINTOSH PLUS's astonishing 2011 debut, *FLORAL SHOPPE*. The only release by Xavier credited to MACINTOSH PLUS, *FLORAL SHOPPE* is an impressively solid album that moves effortlessly between beauty and noise, serenity and disquiet, confusion and transcendence. The album's most famous track, "リサフランク 420 / 現代のコンピュー," could be considered vaporwave in its most refined and classical form: a slowed Diana Ross song chopped and screwed to oblivion, compressed, and interminably catchy. *FLORAL SHOPPE* sounds, as music critic Adam Downer writes, "as though it [is] the internet spitting back what we've been feeding into it"; he calls it "the future's first masterpiece."[34] Indeed, no other album in recent memory so well captures the early twenty-first century as an accelerated, anthrodecentric world quickly becoming more simulated and more digitized with every passing year.

MACINTOSH PLUS and Xavier's other vaporwave projects are the sounds of future shock and techno-decay during the twilight of late capitalism, but for Xavier, the political critique grew from personal experience as a child coming of age in the first decade of the twenty-first century. "I grew up with my dad working at Microsoft for a decade, and [I] grew up isolated," she says, "and I watched the job sort of suck the life force out of him...these companies are destroying us as a society and their employees are just a byproduct."[35] Xavier's story could be the story of many children growing up in the 2000s, with parents chained to the numbing routine of corporate work and the Internet serving as the vista through which a wider community of like-minded people could be reached. Several vaporwave releases, and Xavier's projects specifically, confront this youthful period during the immediate years after 9/11 with both a slight yearning and an incredulous eye. *FLORAL SHOPPE*, for example, is composed of songs and sounds from the 80s and 90s, both times before 9/11 and the rise of the Internet, but by drastically tampering with the samples of these older tunes, Xavier throws the nostalgia "in a centrifuge" and gives us "the colder, more stark side of it."[36]

The result is not only an album for the Internet culture *about* Internet culture but also a startling declaration that opposes Joseph Lanza's simplistic view of recent technological history: capitalism has not delivered us from oppression. All the Muzak, all the consumer goods, all the accessibility – none of these amenities have helped us to swallow the reality that the great deterritorializing force of unrestrained capitalism has wiped any sort of meaning from society. As Alain Badiou reminds us: "Sure, they say, we may not live in a condition of perfect Goodness. But we're lucky that we don't live in a condition of Evil."[37] By lowering our expectations for what a decent, well-mannered society could be, we can then accept whiling away our days in the virtual plaza, taking advantage of what the mega-corporations have to offer and blindly believing the lie that any of us can live the dream as long as we pull ourselves up by the boot straps.

What is not explained in late capitalism is that the entire system is a dream, and *FLORAL SHOPPE* is the sound of that dream as it is – a fantasy world where life accelerates to the point of stasis. "The idea of acclerationism and the singularity resonate with me a lot," Xavier explains, and her music presents the singularity not as a sci-fi narrative with cyborgs living forever in a future utopia but as humans glued to smartphones communicating in tweets while corporatism destroys the planet.[38]

As a contemporary form of music making, vaporwave resists easy categorization as either parody, pastiche, or hauntology. Like one of Hutcheon's parodies, vaporwave subverts and criticizes established norms and *doxa*, but it also belongs to the class of art that draws on the past not only to *critique* it but also to *dismantle* it. It seeks to establish a certain mood or setting – drifting through the virtual plaza, numb and caught in a consumption loop – and is consistently critical of that mood or setting. Like *The Cabin in the Woods* and *Too Many Cooks*, vaporwave is one of these burgeoning artistic forms that seeks to retroactively upend the progress of history by dissolving the notion of temporality altogether or by trashing the icons of our past. What makes vaporwave unique as a new method of Internet-produced punk is its relationship to the sights and sounds of unrestrained capitalism. Vaporwave spits in the face of late capitalism and mocks the very methods used to sell us the things we don't need, all while problematizing our understanding of history.

Chapter 4

Sick and Tired:
9/11 and Regressive Culture
in the Twenty-First Century

Today those who peer into the future want only relief from
anxiety.
– John Gray[1]

It's a hollow play / But they'll clap anyway.
– Arcade Fire, "My Body is a Cage"[2]

There is a startling moment in Jennifer Egan's Pulitzer Prize-
winning novel, A Visit from the Goon Squad, in which a supporting
character, Bix, predicts the technological deliverance and
social rebirth that will, in time, define the Western twenty-first
century. The scene is set in the mid-1990s – change is in the
air and the future looks promising for Bix and his college-aged
friends, Drew and Rob. Drew ruminates on losing touch with
the other two in the near future, but Bix, with his finger on the
technological pulse of the world, tells Drew not to worry:

"Oh, we'll know each other forever," Bix says. "The days of
losing touch are almost gone."
"What does that mean?" Drew asks.
"We're going to meet again in a different place," Bix says.
"Everyone we've lost, we'll find. Or they'll find us."
"Where? How?" Drew asks.
Bix hesitates, like he's held this secret so long he's afraid
of what will happen when he releases it into the air. "I picture
it like Judgment Day," he says finally, his eyes on the water.
"We'll rise up out of our bodies and find each other again in

spirit form. We'll meet in that new place, all of us together, and first it'll seem strange, and pretty soon it'll seem strange that you could ever lose someone, or get lost."[3]

We would eventually all meet again, at that great, everlasting party that is social media, and the true final frontier would be the Internet, on our desktops and laptops and then into our hands and pockets to be accessed at any given time. Suddenly, at the turn of the twenty-first century, all human knowledge was at our fingertips – the good and the bad, the empowering and the grotesque, the stupid and the unspeakable. We would use this great gift of technology to hide from a world too complex, too unforgiving, too "unthinkable," and retreat into a vast land of likes and hashtags, the echo chamber wherein everything resides. At my girlfriend's college graduation I attended recently, I looked around at a stadium filled with parents, grandparents, brothers, sisters, children, and friends all with their smartphones recording the fireworks ending the ceremony and sending the class of 2015 off on its way into the world. This was the scene Bix would have understood, but I could not help but ask myself if this was the world we were hoping for and had envisioned. The smartphone revolution, or the social media boom, or the post-Internet age – whatever you could call it – had happened so fast that no one stopped to ask if it *should* or to ponder the possible ramifications of such ubiquitous information and interconnectivity. And here we all were, recording memories we would later forget to share online with people who barely know us.

But maybe we needed the comfort blanket of a smartphone. After all, for Westerners, history showed itself in all its sound and violent fury on September 11, 2001 and knocked the shell-shocked West back into infancy. In her book *The Shock Doctrine: The Rise of Disaster Capitalism*, Naomi Klein outlines the shocks, both man-made and otherwise, that have led to totalitarian capitalism's victory as the reigning ideology of our time. Klein's model of history is littered with these shocks, which knock entire countries into regressive states of disorientation, but it is 9/11 that provides Klein with her most terrifying form of shock therapy:

> Suddenly we found ourselves living in a kind of Year Zero, in which everything we knew of the world before could now be dismissed as "pre-9/11 thinking." Never strong in our knowledge of history, North Americans had become a blank slate – "a clean sheet of paper" on which "the newest and most beautiful words can be written," as Mao said of his people. A new army of experts instantly materialized to write new and beautiful words on the receptive canvas of our posttrauma consciousness: "clash of civilizations," they inscribed. "Axis of evil," "Islamo-fascism," "homeland security." With everyone preoccupied by the deadly new culture wars, the Bush administration was able to pull off what it could only have dreamed of doing before 9/11: wage privatized wars abroad and build a corporate security complex at home.[4]

Writing on the eve of the 2008 financial crisis and subsequent massive bailout, Klein could only predict the strange culture wars that would continue into the second decade of the twenty-first century. By exploding the world as we knew it, the September 11th attacks shocked us into a state of cultural regression. We have been living in that period ever since, plumbing the past for comforting sounds and songs, sounds from the periphery and mundanity of daily life before the great unraveling at the start of this century. The second hook to the jaw of America came in 2008 as the collapse of the economy rendered the myth of capitalism a bit harder to swallow and as Barack Obama, the progressive hope for a society that had lived through the dark age of George W. Bush, cowed before the Wall Street fat cats and then continued Bush's hawkish tactics to police the world and erase the enemy with his ruthless drone strikes.

The shock of 9/11 was the shock of the Real, rearing its ugly head for all to see, and its arrival sounded the end of a century rife with spectacular horrors and stunning injustice. "In contrast to the nineteenth century of utopian or 'scientific' projects and ideals," theorist Slavoj Zizek writes, "the twentieth century aimed at delivering the thing itself – at directly realizing the longed-for New Order. The ultimate and defining moment of the twentieth century was the direct experience of the Real as opposed to everyday social reality – the Real in its extreme violence as the price to be paid for peeling off the deceptive layers of reality."[5]

Writing shortly after 9/11, Zizek muses on the cultural and political ramifications of such an expression of the Real in a new century and predicts our collective regression thereafter. "Now, in the months following the attacks," he writes, "it is as if we are living in the unique time between a traumatic event and its symbolic impact, as in those brief moments after we have been deeply cut, before the full extent of the pain strikes us."[6] Echoing Klein's metaphor of the shock, Zizek notes that directly after 9/11 the dismay was palpable. "In the traumatic aftermath of September 11," he continues, "when the old security seemed to be momentarily shattered, what could be more 'natural' than taking refuge in the innocence of a firm ideological identification?"[7] Thus, he identifies Americans' renewed faith in the symbolic gestures of patriotism, like the parading of American flags, after foreign terror cracked the veneer of Western capitalist complacency.[8] Suddenly, these symbols of nationalistic pride rang true again, and Americans banded together under an "us vs. them" banner. Forget the past decades of American exceptionalism at the expense of other countries. We were harmed by them.

The dread that formed over American culture drove us back inside our houses, hands over our heads in fear of the Real, eventually turning to the Internet and social media to hide away from the terror waiting in the wings. "What awaits us is something much more uncanny: the spectre of an 'immaterial' war where the attack is invisible," writes Zizek, channeling the atmospheric, unnamable horror that permeates modern culture – the notion that *something* has gone awry, something nebulous and foreboding, a mood present in such pop-culture phenomena as the aforementioned *True Detective*.[9] Our present situation in the United States – with systemic racial violence, right-wing terrorism, ecological destruction, and economic turmoil – is becoming too volatile to ignore, yet the culture industry still peddles ludicrous, infantile fantasies and has done so for decades. But after 9/11 it is the rampant "retromania," as Simon Reynolds calls it, that is perhaps the most harmful to our culture.

Simon Reynolds' *Retromania: Pop Culture's Addiction to Its Own Past* is as much a critique of the culture industry as it is a scathing takedown of contemporaneity – always plugged in, surface-level, distracted, frantic, and bored. Nostalgia is nothing new, according to Reynolds, and in fact, musicians and label execs alike have been drawing on the icons of the past to sell records for decades. But Reynolds sees the Internet as the ultimate fulfillment of our desire for the wholesale consumption of culture. We binge on music until we no longer have an appetite left, and then we hide in the labyrinth of the Internet where we can be whoever we want.

Reynolds is leery of what the iPod and the Internet have done to our capacity to actually reside in the present. Because we have access to everything all the time, "it is a struggle to recall that life wasn't always like this; that relatively recently, one lived most of the time in a cultural present tense, with the past confined to specific zones, trapped in particular objects and locations."[10] Instead, as we consume as much information as the Internet can allow, we enter into a digital feeding frenzy where we fear the prospect of missing out on checking the latest Instagram post, reading the latest music review, or hearing the latest single. For Reynolds, the MP3 is the "ideal format for an era where current music, with its high-turnover micro-trends and endless giveaway podcasts and DJ mixes, is increasingly something you *keep up with*" (his italics).[11] Music has become the most troublesome cultural commodity, the one that has companies like Spotify and Apple scrambling to solve music piracy while ushering in what journalist David Carr calls the "perfect world" in which "the consumer wants all the music that he or she desires – on demand, at a cost of zero or close to it."[12]

In this oversaturated culture, we feed on media to a point beyond fullness, and that can open up within the most avid media junkie an "abyss," as Reynolds calls it, "the dimensions of which are in proportion to the emptiness of your life."[13] Perhaps we can think of it as digital melancholia, the feeling of never being full, of never encountering an end to the information stream, of never actually catching up with all that culture we feel we must keep up with in the first place. It is a lonely, exhausting burden unique to our moment in history. After all, you are still alone in your room even after checking Facebook, downloading a trove of music, and watching pornography. This bitter loneliness, one that gives the illusion of socializing on these social media platforms, is a facet of this digital melancholia: we surf the web alone and binge on media alone.

What lasting effects does this digital melancholia have on us as a society *and* as individual human beings? Tracing the psychological and neurological effects of digital-media consumption is a topic for another book entirely, yet there are numerous studies that illustrate what the Internet has done to our brains.[14] Reynolds points to attention-deficit disorder as one symptom of our manic, plugged-in, social-media-obsessed culture and notes that ADD, "like so many ailments and dysfunctions under late capitalism...[is] caused by the environment, in this case the datascape."[15] When faced with an infinite amount of information and, in this case, music, you will never be able to feed on it all, but our blind faith in technology under late capitalism has allowed for companies like Apple to assuage us of the anxiety of choice with inventions like the iPod. Reynolds is particularly critical of the iPod's shuffle function, which "relieves you of the burden of desire itself." Going further, Reynolds describes the typical music consumer in the iPod age as "omnivorous, non-partisan, promiscuously eclectic, drifting indolently across the sea of commodified sound."[16] This is the description of the hipster elite, one that treats culture as a commodity and seeks to use the accumulation of cultural capital as an indication of knowledge.

Reynolds outlines a step-by-step process by which we arrived at this point in music history:

First music was reified, turned into a thing (vinyl records, analogue tapes) you could buy, store, keep under your own personal control. Then music was 'liquefied,' turned into data that could be streamed, carried anywhere, transferred between different devices. With the MP3, music became a devalued currency in two senses: there was just too much of it (as with hyper-inflation, banks printing too much money), but also because of the way it flowed into people's lives like a current or fluid. This made music start to resemble a utility (like water or electricity) as opposed to an artistic experience whose temporality you subjected yourself to. Music has become a continuous supply that is fatally susceptible to discontinuity (pause, rewind/fast-forward, save for later, and so forth).[17]

I would argue that there is a third step in this process – vaporization. Music transforms from a "thing" into a stream and then finally into a formless cloud that infiltrates our everyday. This is different from the piped-in Muzak of prior decades. Vaporized music is the music of PR, the sound of ephemeral, hollow music. It is music you encounter, not music you listen to – in Internet advertisements, in clubs and bars, in grocery stores and malls. It is not meant to soothe you or to help you perform better at your day job or to necessarily sell you something. This is the sound of hype, of constant streams of music criticism evaluating albums and posting their declaration of worth within days of release. The vaporization of music makes it easier to sell of course, but the goal is to shape public opinion. With social media sites and mainstream music outlets parroting one another's opinions, there is no longer any room for a differing opinion. Either you subscribe to the monolithic opinion of a hyped band or you are simply a contrarian, and the best part is you don't even have to listen to the music being discussed to join the chorus of prevailing opinions.

The result is an all-consuming music culture prone to buying into hype and regressive fantasies while shunning dissenting opinions. Our post-9/11 Internet culture is more interested in "[escaping] the here-and-now, the bland suburban everyday...through fantasy (the tremendous popularity of novels and movies based around magic, vampires, wizardry, the supernatural) or digital technology."[18] As Hollywood doles out one superhero movie after another and the teen romantic-fantasy book genre delivers endless dreck, our culture becomes total fantasy, one without acknowledgement of our current place in history – which is characterized by rampant unemployment and underemployment, staggering debt, a diminishing middle class, racial injustice, transphobia, environmental disaster, and emotionally and intellectually stunted political groups paid by massive corporations to perpetuate fantasies in order to dilute the collective consciousness of the West.

"I think it's a rather alarming sign if we've got audiences of adults going to see the *Avengers* movie and delighting in concepts and characters meant to entertain the 12-year-old boys of the 1950s," quips Alan Moore, writer of such acclaimed comics as *Watchmen* and *Lost Girls*.[19] The explosion of superhero movies dominating the mainstream American cinema is only a piece of the larger cultural regression into modes of safe, digestible fantasy, and writers like Moore argue this turn towards mythic narratives meant to ease us into false complacency is frightening – especially in a time of social and political distress. It is also a sign of cultural collapse, of the culture industry eating itself like the ancient ouroboros. Pulitzer Prize-winning author Chris Hedges thinks it is ultimately a harbinger of the end:

The last days of any civilization, when populations are averting their eyes from the unpleasant realities before them, become carnivals of hedonism and folly. Rome went down like this. So did the Ottoman and Austro-Hungarian Empires. Men and women of stunning mediocrity and depravity assume political control. Today charlatans and hucksters hold forth on the airwaves, and intellectuals are ridiculed. Force and militarism, with their hypermasculine ethic, are celebrated. And the mania for hope requires the silencing of any truth that is not childishly optimistic.[20]

This passage is taken from Hedges' *Wages of Rebellion*, a firestorm of critical vitriol hurled at contemporaneity and its discontents. In the book, Hedges surveys the history of civilization and notes that American society is mimicking the last days of several prominent and powerful societies. Neoliberal capitalism, Hedges argues, has surpassed its tipping point. It is time for thoughtful rebellion. We can no longer continue to lower our standards in order to live in simulated reality and widespread subjugation. Unfettered capitalism must be replaced.

But it seems that the easier solution is the most harmful. By studying culture in the twenty-first century, I understand now that the collective impulse to bury our heads in the sand is much easier to do than resisting the powers that be. And the tendrils of capital have already snaked their way into our nostalgia. Now, even our desire to escape and retreat into the past is commodified.

Happier Ghosts: A Better World Back Then

As we have seen before, cultural nostalgia is strongest with regards to our technology boom. We pine for analog technology and readily consume the myth that we can hide safely in the pre-digital warmth of the past's media technologies. In the early 2010's, vaporwave began its ascent from the digital underground, and by the release of Taylor Swift's 2014 amnesiac epic, *1989*, past-baiting had become mainstream. A notable example of this is the song "Lonely Town," Brandon Flowers' single from his 2015 album, *The Desired Effect*. The song by the Killers' front man is unabashedly retro and lyrically draws on youthful exuberance and memory ("Spinning like a Gravitron when I was just a kid. / I always thought things would change, but they never did."), but the music video is the most troubling aspect of the song. In it, a teenage girl puts a cassette of Flowers' album into her Walkman, places the headphones on her head, and then dances to "Lonely Town" by herself in her house. The icons of a pre-digital period in history are all present: the Walkman, the dated furniture, the corded telephone, and the handwritten note from her parents ("Help yourself to the fridge! Please take out trash!"). The imagery is indicative of some time before "now" yet still vague enough to resist a specific time period. Instead the video is set in "the past" – an unclear "everywhen" that mashes up

80s and 90s iconography. Her awkward dance moves and uninhibited sense of carefree enjoyment is punctuated by the startling revelation that she is entirely alone. No cell phones, no social media, and no one else around her until the very end when the video turns from a simple dance montage into a cheeky homage to 80s slasher movies. Suddenly we as viewers take on the role of the onlooker outside her house, but the change in perspective to participatory voyeur does more than just allude to 80s horror cinema. Instead we creepily become what we already are – yearning eyes staring through a window into our fantasy of what we think the past was. We become something like the killer in *Too Many Cooks* – an intrusive outsider thirsty for the youthful flesh of the dancing girl's naïveté. The music video reinforces our culture's dream of the past as simpler, more childish, and all-around better than the present. Her vulnerability manifests itself through her dancing, and not once does a distraction wrench her from her moment of bliss.

Take note again of the aforementioned lyric: "I always thought things would change, but they never did." "Lonely Town" can be read as a song about historical alternatives, and the video portrays an alternate present where the digital boom of ubiquitous technology never took place. As a culture, we delight in feeding on this myth, yet in a way we are living through it. The Internet allows the past to be easily consumed at any time, and apps like Instagram turn our smartphones into shoddy replicas of dated cameras in order to give us the feeling we're consuming the real thing. We can copy the fashion trends of the 80s and 90s and even create derivative art that reproduces the sights and sounds of the past, but we have difficulty giving up our addiction to information in order to dive fully into the world presented in the "Lonely Town" video. Instead we live in a time without time when the past ceaselessly haunts the present – a fantasy world in which we can utilize the endless capabilities of digital technology while copping the visual imagery of previous decades.

Vaporwave is an excellent example of just how commodified the ghosts of our past are. The earliest vaporwave producers sought to recontextualize our insatiable hunger for the past by delivering nostalgia in its remembered form – hazy, looping, distorted, unclear – all while mocking and subverting the entire process. Throughout vaporwave's brief but rapid evolution, it has diverged into two primary artistic modes. The first is a blend of the vaporwave aesthetic with more contemporary beats and production and is often associated with acts such as the Fresno-based producer Blank Banshee. The other resembles the classic form of vaporwave (repetition, pitched samples, little post-production) but is sometimes presented in a more concentrated form. For instance, take the 2014 vaporwave album *Telenights* by g h o s t i n g released on the Dream Catalogue label. *Telenights* is one of many albums released so far on this prolific vaporwave platform, yet it stands out for its unabashed presentation of various late-night TV commercials and programs with little in the way of post-production. Unlike an album such as *MIDNIGHT TELEVISION*, another homage to late-night television and hypnagogic pop, *Telenights* rarely makes use of jagged editing or even the kind of mind-numbing repetition found on *MIDNIGHT TELEVISION*'s "Blind Dates." Instead, *Telenights* plays like channel surfing while falling asleep, with its scattered samples of consumer electronics commercials, Halloween special bumpers, and Late Movie adverts ostensibly from the 1980s and 90s. Little is known about g h o s t i n g, whose name recalls both the particular form of television interference and the smartphone-era "phenomenon" of breaking off a relationship by pulling a digital disappearing act, yet the only album so far attached to the project delivers straight, undiluted lo-fi nostalgia that draws on the techniques of classic vaporwave producers while refining them. In many ways, *Telenights* is the paramount Romantic album of the vaporwave genre – an awe-inspiring collection of pre-digital television in its natural mundanity. It is the sound of near-pure nostalgia and of the media industry's refusal to sleep even when we have to.

Make Haste to Collapse

There is, however, a flipside to artists like g h o s t i n g – producers that mirror the anticipation and dread of the accelerating future rather than complicate our idea of the past. The genre is often called distroid, and its musical practitioners employ the sounds and imagery of contemporary electronic pop with its blasting drums, Autotuned vocals, and club synths. The result is something like robotic trap played in humanity's last club on the eve of the apocalypse. Distroid is the music of an accelerating culture, the soundtrack of a society careening off the rails towards total collapse.

"Accelerationism is the notion that the dissolution of civilisation wrought by capitalism should not and cannot be resisted," musicologist Adam Harper writes, "but rather must be pushed faster and farther towards the insanity and anarchically fluid violence that is its ultimate conclusion, either because this is liberating, because it causes a revolution, or because destruction is the only logical answer."[21] Pulling from the philosophical writings of Nick Land and Gilles Deleuze, Harper makes the case that distroid is the underground's answer to "contemporary hi-tech 'overground' subcultural pop" that has become the mainstream norm.[22] Distroid outfits such as Principles and James Ferraro's BEBETUNE$ and BODYGUARD projects dabble in frantic, gleaming hi-fi music that is both caffeinated and idiotic. Distroid is the alternate form of escape from this neoliberal dystopia. We can either hide away in the appropriated iconography of mythic pre-9/11 naïveté or dope up on the "intensely macho...post-human...[and] thrillingly alien" jungle juice of contemporary pop music, with its ageist themes of vapid club drama.[23]

Principles' aptly named *Candy Brain* consists of eleven hi-fi stadium-ready electro-pop songs that sound like an amped-up remix of Rustie's *Glass Swords* (2011) or the slew of maximalist bubblegum cyber-pop found on the PC Music label. It is music for the addled mind on Ritalin, a blasting sugary onslaught that is less macho than BODYGUARD but just as schizophrenic. The album, with its front cover of a skull-faced lollipop, scans as an infantile version of distroid, but functions in arguably the same way as BODYGUARD's *Silica Gel* mixtape, which Adam Harper calls "the gruesome logical endpoint of a culture that pushes body supplementation and modification products and their ideologies well beyond the point of inhumanity."[24] Distroid is our distracted and rapid environment in its most literal form – the celebration of chaos and mental illness at the expense of the body.

Music Sickness

Though they exist on opposite ends, both g h o s t i n g and BODYGUARD operate on the same spectrum, one that seeks to upend the established musical order with its relentless PR and capitalistic concerns. They both mock contemporary culture's ludicrous fantasies by exhibiting the darker, more subversive sides of those collective delusions and they embrace the idea that perhaps we have reached an "end" to music as anything other than a product pushed by a corporatized media complex. Popular music cranked out by media giants is everywhere, and the bulk of it is asinine. The diluted form of songwriting populating mainstream radio and consumed by the masses has perhaps caused us to lash out at music's supposed function in our lives. If it is something we keep up with, as Simon Reynolds points out, and if the majority of it is mindless fodder, than perhaps we have reached a crossroads.

There is no coincidence that vaporwave as a genre can be considered a reaction to our possible sickness of music. Dream Catalogue founder, known as Hong Kong Express, spoke of his dissatisfaction with music in general during an interview with Red Bull:

> I was actually sick and tired of music for many years before I discovered vaporwave...Even though I had loved music since I was a kid, I was entirely sick of it for a long time, and I actually went months at a time without even listening to any at all. I became really bitter about music in general which was fueled by the general depression I had...Vaporwave really rekindled my love for music, to the point where I enjoy it as much as I did when I was a teenager.[25]

HKE goes on to describe a previous discussion he had with a producer who goes by the moniker IMMUNE//:

> Earlier today, [IMMUNE//] described vapor to me as "the end of music," which I found quite poignant. And I think what he was getting at is this being not only the end of music, but the beginning of a new way of experiencing it.[26]

HKE's resolution offers hope for a musically drained culture, and he does not stand alone in feeling bloated from the massive information binge the Internet can allow. Others have taken note of a supposed information fullness, a loss of appetite when it comes to more media, more music, more content. Stephen Thompson, writing for NPR's *The Good Listener* program, grapples with the question: "...do you ever get sick of music?"[27] That means listening to it, reading about it, and generally encountering it day to day. Writing on the heels of U2's *Songs of Innocence* release, an album the band uploaded to Apple users' iTunes account without permission, Thompson declares we should take a break from music every once in a while to keep sane, a sentiment that sounds quite similar to the glut of online articles urging us to "go dark" and unplug from distractive technology every so often.

It's not hard to see that people are genuinely concerned with their feelings towards music. Maybe we are consuming too much, as Simon Reynolds thinks, due to endless torrenting and downloading. Maybe the major labels have mastered the art of daily infiltration, forcibly reminding us of their latest signee and the highest-charting pop single. U2, once a band that undermined popular culture in much the same way vaporwave does, joined forces with Apple to circumvent the very choosing and buying process of music in order to meld advertising with consumption. *Songs of Innocence* sitting in our iTunes accounts casually prompts us that U2 has a new album *and* that we ostensibly want it. It is both product and advertisement in one, the erasure of musical integrity at the hands of industry.

"Everything happens so much," Lindsay Zoladz of Pitchfork reminds us, and there is too much music to process.[28] On top of that, the mainstream music industry insists on lowering the cultural bar by pushing artists whose music is both catchy and annoying, fun and mindless – derivative, hackneyed, formulaic, and worth millions. Turn on contemporary country radio, and you will find inane copies of the same clichéd song sung by various singers, whether it's the subtly creepy "Who Are You When I'm Not Looking" by Blake Shelton or RaeLynn's chaste-girl fantasy, "God Made Girls," or anything dredged up by Florida Georgia Line. At this point, it would not take much to write country music on something higher than a sixth-grade level. It's almost difficult to come up with the same recycled cud without copping an entire song word for word and note for note (though that seems to be happening anyway in the pop arena – just look at singer Ariana Grande's "Problem," a blatant, how-is-this-legal ripoff of C+C Music Factory's "Gonna Make You Sweat").

Country-music writers in the twenty-first century produce songs marketed almost solely for southern, white, Christian conservatives, but it's not only these far-right, jejune anthems of reductionism that push us away from music. Consider the Mercury Prize-winning alt-J (or Δ, if you will), a band about as far removed from Luke Bryan as possible while still remaining mainstream; yet these guys from Leeds and most contemporary country music occupy two sides of the same coin. alt-J has been called "awesome" (Drowned in Sound),[29] "smart" (NME),[30] and "beautiful" (BBC Music),[31] as well as "overstuffed" (Pitchfork)[32] and "a band that finds itself at the top after failing upward and has no idea what their next step is" (Pitchfork again).[33] So maybe they are not universally acclaimed, but this is a band whose sophomore album, *This Is All Yours*, peaked at number one on the *Billboard* Top Rock Albums chart in the fall of 2014[34] and who writes lyrics such as, "Turn you inside out and lick you like a crisp packet," "In your snatch fits pleasure, broom-shaped pleasure," and perhaps their most meaningless line, "Me, I'm in bin / Ignore her worth and some trivia."[35]

alt-J is the left's equivalent of conservative country music, but instead of offensively simplistic illusions of God creating girls because "[s]omebody's gotta wear a pretty skirt," alt-J proffers utter lyrical nonsense and fratty dubstep synth lines disguised as obliquely hip, trailblazing music whose only forebear is Radiohead.[36] If alt-J is the band of the mid-2010s deemed worthy of a comparison to Radiohead, then I guess I am sick of music as well.

But maybe we are sicker of music writing and criticism than of music itself. After all it's partially the fault of the music press that some opening act at amateur night like alt-J is hyped up to be our next band to raise the musical bar. In their piece for Tiny Mix Tapes entitled "The Trouble with Contemporary Music

Criticism," James Parker and Nicholas Croggon explain why music criticism has not only eclipsed our actual enjoyment and individual evaluation of music but also morphed into something like hashtag criticism. They term this form of music writing, the kind that pops up the most online where anything can be referenced and hyperlinked, "retro-historicism," "historical list-making," and "influence fishing."[37] These music sites write reviews that engage in "mere identification and cataloguing of historical reference points before moving on to pass judgment, as if that were in any way sufficient."[38]

"This type of review says so little it might as well read: #ChewedCorners #Paradinas #chillwave #italodisco #pianohouse #hiphop #hardcore #footwork #UKfunky #house = 7.1/10," Parker and Croggon write, and their insight is spot-on.[39] Retrohistoricist reviewing does little more than offer a series of terms to joggle our addled, harried memories into thinking, "Oh, this is good because it references krautrock."

This is reactionary music criticism for reactionary music, the kind that capitalizes on our nostalgia for lost or even lived-through times, and these retro-historicist publications hype bands for their nostalgia-baiting. They ignore progressivism in favor of conventional bands that do what Simon Reynolds hates the most: keep the past-gazing and lose the pain of memory to garner popularity.

At the Endless Mall

Vaporwave is one genre that problematizes this entire system of lazy critical evaluation, often just by remaining left out of these publications altogether, and its avoidance can be attributed to the genre's skeptical and mocking relationship with history. "Vaporwave is democratic because, in principle, anyone could do it," Parker and Croggon continue. "At its most basic — which is also to say at its most radical — vaporwave consists of nothing more than an act of reframing, normally of some chintzy piece of forgotten muzak dredged up from the depths of the web."[40] This is vaporwave's unique strength in a musical climate so taken with safety and familiarity. The producers making simple, radical vaporwave dissolve the notion of progress both in its creation and in the feelings it invokes in us. It is music that sheds new light on history instead of trying to make sense of some kind of easy-to-understand historical progression.

Sadly, the reigning opinions of the mainstream music press dictate the tastes that we buy into. Any sort of challenging notion is usually entirely ignored, like vaporwave. The result can be considered a monoculture in which we must continue to laud the typical titans of the music industry trotted out before us by a dying label system or suffer the backlash of public consensus.

With the release of Taylor Swift's *1989*, we have finally arrived at the moment when Western popular music eats itself whole, when radical thought and progressivism collapse under our infantilized awe and uncritical acceptance of so-called liberating technologism and material illusion, when the loaded eye of social media watches our rehearsed reaction to corporatized artistic tripe. "In a society that seeks constant validation through social media, '1989' serves as a conformist power fantasy that might resonate more than we'd like to admit," Chris Richards writes for *The Washington Post*, "because it's also a big, dull gesture we're expected to applaud no matter what. Clap a little louder or be excommunicated to the valley of the haters. Those are your options in this ludicrous world."[41]

Richards ends his article with an impassioned cry, the sound of one critic refusing to jump on the critical bandwagon and trust in the Instagramming of pop music:

Is it wrong to wish "1989" didn't sound so anonymous? Is it wrong to demand our leaders not make follower music? Is it wrong to feel disoriented and disheartened by the effusion of suck-uppy articles dutifully praising these unimaginative songs? Is it wrong to squirm knowing that those same songs will likely saturate our public spaces for years – or maybe even the rest of our lives?[42]

It is not wrong. And it is quite terrifying knowing that we will either kill ourselves economically or ecologically while repeating the mantra of memory erasure: "Shake It Off." 1989 is now the year two concurrent ideologies took hold: unfettered capitalism and Taylor Swift. One was born from the other. Both signal the end of history and the era of amnesia. Are there no alternatives?

"Taylor Swift...flattened New York City – by rendering it utterly banal – in a way no terrorists ever could," writes critic Ryan Alexander Diduck in his 2014 recap for *The Quietus*, "and penned 'Blank Space,' the most heartfelt inadvertent ode to disaster capitalism in recent memory."[43] But none of this matters once you slap a filter over it all. Our limitless nostalgia, our willingness to subscribe to an ideology that scrambles our codes of meaning in exchange for material pleasure, our addiction to information, and our distracted, regressive tendencies form the base of a greater societal crisis – a general failure of the future. The ghosts of the past, with their optimistic vision of the future, are welcome guests in our mausoleum culture, in which we enslave them (as Simon Reynolds notes) in order to revisit a time before now.

I can remember first hearing my friends, most of them in their early twenties, talk about "giving up." Why continue? They would ask, why try to fight or hope for a better future when this one arrived as an utter failure? Many of us took to the welcoming playground of the Internet to live in a perpetual-info bliss where we can be whomever we want and scroll through the visual iconography of the past. Consider the *hikikomori*, the Japanese term for adolescents who move in with their parents and shut themselves away from the outside world. These young people, for a variety of reasons, would rather live out their lives in online solitude than put up with an insane world that sucks them dry and leaves them empty. The images of rooms wherein *hikikomori* live are cluttered with books, comics, snack food, laptops, televisions, magazines, et cetera, and some experts clock the number of *hikikomori* living in Japan at one million mostly male young people.[44]

We are all becoming cultural *hikikomori*, more concerned with staying within the cocoon of our media fortresses and terrified of the larger world and its exploits. This is not our fault. Living in a globalized, economically destitute society has turned us into neurotic Internet-dwellers with our nerves relentlessly racked by political failures and a media industry that runs on the fumes of our panic and anxiety. We do everything we can, from colorfully invoking a better world on Instagram to adopting the fashion trends of a vague past era, to distract us from the existential reality that under late capitalism we are miserable.[45]

Are we doomed to a future in which we yearn for the clichés of the past to ease our anxious, frantic minds and bloated, cancerous bodies? Do we now plead aloud like the *Washington Post*'s Chris Richards for something new, something real, something left untainted by the tendrils of capital to invade our culture and awaken us from this narcotized fever dream? Can we no longer recognize that our very nostalgia for a time before globalized capitalism is being commodified and sold back to us? Or as long as the wolf is kept from the door, do we settle for these stunted cultural norms that celebrate regression and, when consumed, wipe our memories like the waters of Lethe? Do we even want anything "new" anymore?

There is someone out there who can better put forth a manifesto for a new politics of music. This book was not meant to do that. Instead, its goal was to take a hard look at a tiny flash-point in culture, the birth of vaporwave, and to situate it within our contemporary moment – one characterized by uncanny ghosts, historical trauma, regression, simulation, and a nebulous strangeness that seems to hum menacingly underneath it all.

As I mentioned in the introduction, listening to vaporwave, an alternative to both the mainstream music and media industries, is one way to resist these massive complexes that promote hype and image and run on profit – very often at the expense of the music itself. Several aesthetic elements of vaporwave are seeping into the mainstream, yet its political sting, its jarring indictment of consumerist culture, must not disappear even at the mainstream level. And vaporwave's act of reframing our history, of allowing us to revisit the corporate music of previous decades and to re-evaluate its emotional appeal, must also not be forgotten because it accomplishes something contemporary music rarely does. It invites us to react emotionally to a genre of music that has subversive potential. There is so much music being made to lull us into indifference and to help us escape from the monotony of everyday life, but there must be those who throw us back into the world, who do not commodify our ghosts, who force us to look at the wider injustices, and who artistically wrestle with this alienating, unbalanced, unstable racket we call Western society.

For now, we live in the mall, but I think it's closing soon. There are forces outside breaking through the glass, threatening to interrupt this dream we're drifting through, doped on consumer goods, energy drinks, and Apple products, climbing toward the bright light of digital deliverance. If they can break through in time, there may be a way to save us, and then we can shut off the assembly-line music that's being piped through these grand halls of commerce. Maybe they'll tear the whole charade down, and we can wake up enough to mobilize, to make plans for an unsimulated world, to instruct our children to never settle for life in the haunted mall. There is a way out of this cultural nightmare.

Afterword

The Vapor Decade

We can mark the beginning and the end of the 2010s with Kevin Allocca. Global Director of Culture and Trends at YouTube, Allocca achieved fame with his 2011 TED Talk, "Why Videos Go Viral," in which he explained the three factors determining whether a video will go viral: tastemakers, communities of participation, and unexpectedness.

First, for a video to go viral in the early 2010s, a tastemaker, like a celebrity or a talk show host, needed to tweet about it or talk about it on their show. Allocca's example was the former hit commentary show *Tosh.0*, hosted by comedian Daniel Tosh, who poked fun at the most ridiculous videos posted to YouTube each week, fueling their virality. Then, after a major figure platformed the video, different communities would remix it in their own way. His example was *Nyan Cat*, a looped animated video of a flying cat with a Pop-Tart body spewing rainbow colors behind it. At the time, it seemed everyone had their own take on *Nyan Cat*: there was the smooth jazz version, the ragtime version, and French, Japanese, Russian, and American iterations. Anyone anywhere could join the *Nyan Cat* trend by making their own. Finally, Allocca contended that only the most unexpected and unique videos uploaded to YouTube would ever go viral. World famous tastemakers and remixing communities can amplify a video, but only that which is "totally surprising and humorous," he said, will circulate widely.

In 2011, Allocca thought that the viral culture of YouTube was the birth of a new, democratic form of creativity, "where anyone has access and the audience defines the popularity." The video of his TED Talk helped to popularize this now debunked notion of social media as an inclusive and equalizing space where all voices can compete and where a silly video could propel anyone to stardom. The idea may seem out of touch to us now, but in the early 2010s Allocca's explanation was one of many claiming social media to be the end of the older culture industry and the beginning of digital democracy.

I used to show the video in my public speaking class because, from a compositional perspective, Allocca's speech is airtight. But each semester the video made less and less sense to my students and to me. It became a relic of another time, an old curiosity. I found myself explaining it to my class not as an example of solid speechwriting but as a window into an older time, when digital platforms were being heralded as the arrival of a long-awaited future. Allocca's enthusiasm and starry-eyed embrace of this "future" is out of place in our time now, and rewatching it reminds me of just how dystopian the early 2010s were.

It was a time when Big Tech marshaled all its resources to convince everyone to buy into the idea that personal growth and responsibility could only happen with a smartphone in hand, and that the future of being social would be mediated. Having friends would mean keeping up with them remotely, watching a highlight reel of their lives posted online. Media companies like TED featured speakers who spread the idea that ideas should spread, that information wants to be free, and that, like Allocca said in his talk, wearing a millennial smart casual outfit of graphic tee and blazer, laughing at a video on YouTube was akin to civic participation. Against this backdrop was a noxious current of nostalgia, itself a reaction to the dizzying rush of digital acceleration and a distraction from the various atrocities of the Bush era that were still being committed under the Obama administration.

It was in this climate that I wrote *Babbling Corpse: Vaporwave and the Commodification of Ghosts*, a contextualization of the vaporwave genre within this strange time period, when horrific realities were often hidden behind the gloss of digital progress. To me, vaporwave mocked the End of History 2.0, when centrist elites celebrated the arrival of a colorblind society emancipated through social media and memes.

While I was writing the book, I came across this Tumblr called "Where Is The Protest Music?" It posted articles that were all asking the same question: Why, in an era of such injustice, weren't major artists being openly political in their music? I've not been able to find the Tumblr since the mid-2010s, but I've come across some of the articles it featured from BBC, *Toronto Star*, and *Salon*. All of them admitted that protest music *was* being written — you just had to know where to find it. But the articles also marveled at the lack of protest animus in mainstream music, or they lamented the possibility that pop music will never galvanize the public to resist the powers that be. Whether there was mainstream protest music in the early-to-mid-2010s is beside the point. For the average listener it certainly felt that way. But the fact that articles were written asking this question points to a larger issue with the time period: that something sinister was hiding behind all the TED talks and Apple events.

To me, vaporwave was a form of musical protest. I had heard nothing else like it in early 2012, when I first came across *FLORAL SHOPPE*, the brilliant, haunting album from MACINTOSH PLUS. You couldn't dance to it; there were no bass drops so popular among both EDM artists and indie bands at the time. It wasn't Pete Seeger either, but it offered a different kind of critique of power, one specific to the birth of the digital age and that resonated with listeners who grew up in malls and supermarkets and came of age online. When every blog-hyped band was ditching guitars for 80s synthesizers, vaporwave reframed nostalgia as something surreal, libidinal, hallucinatory, dare I even say psychedelic. Everything else sounded too awake, too present. *FLORAL SHOPPE* nailed the feeling of in-betweenness: between waking and sleeping, between male and female, between nostalgia and abject horror.

While so many others danced to Cut Copy and Neon Indian, you could drift to vaporwave. You could lose yourself in its repetition, its hypnagogic fog. It was a different kind of bodily experience than listening to the EDM being produced at the time. The Americanized genre of brostep produced by Skrillex and Bassnecter, with its infamous beat drops, was indeed an embodied experience. But the EDM body was often rendered masculine and ableist. When Skrillex posted a link to his favorite song of all time, the airy IDM classic "Flim" by Aphex Twin, the top comments all asked where the drop was. The sonic drop made so famous by Skrillex also mirrored the economic drop of the time, the sound of capitalism revving up then plummeting to dizzying, molar-shaking depths. Emasculated by the Great Recession and feeling uncoupled from their bodies thanks to digital dependence, many sought embodiment through the drop. It was the perfect gimmick to soundtrack market collapse.

And the gear needed to produce EDM could be expensive, too. Which meant only certain artists could afford them. Vaporwave, on the other hand, seemed to be produced on pirated software, with relatively simple editing techniques. In other words vaporwave could be made by anyone, or that's how the music presented itself. The earliest vaporwave releases sampled sounds that could be found online or stashed away in a forgotten media bin somewhere, sounds such as corporate muzak, 80s advertisement bumpers, lite rock, and VHS tapes. And the vaporwave community was a kind of internet underground with a DIY ethos. Monikers obscured authorial intent. How many producers were there really? Or was one person behind them all? Perhaps no humans were involved. Perhaps vaporwave was just the sound of the internet singing back to us.

And what does the internet sound like? The famous treatment of Toto's "Africa" in "Eccojam A1," from Daniel Lopatin's *Chuck Person's Eccojams Vol. 1*, takes the maudlin hook — "Hurry boy, she's waiting there for you" — and chops it into oblivion, the earworm conjured into a coiling serpent, looping and venomous. But vaporwave isn't all abject terror. The euphoric first half of "Eccojam A3" repeats the refrain from Jojo's 2006 hit "Too Little, Too Late." Listening to it is entrancing. It zeroes in on a momentary lift of the song and never lets up. There is so much drama and ecstasy in that one line: "Be real, it doesn't matter anyway/ You know it's just too little, too late." What might have been considered an empty pop phrase meant to convey anything to anyone is now revived, its zombie-like repetition giving it a second life, imbuing it with the passion of the machine. It also made me love Jojo's original in a way I never had before.

Vaporwave voices are recontextualized as something far more alien than their source material, and less binary. Slowed down or sped up, the voices fall somewhere in between masculine and feminine tenors, and without these inflections the vaporwave voice liberates the codings of gender in these older pop songs. Pop music often tries to serve as an escape from one's self, but it doesn't always achieve this; traditional voicings in the cisnormative pop music of the past can trap listeners more firmly in gender performances. Listening to the past can reinscribe all those gender norms so anxiously performed, so firmly entrenched, in the present. By slowing down or speeding up the voices of the past, vaporwave playfully subverts the norms of yesteryear, making fluid what so many in power tried to keep straight, showing us that pop music can indeed de-essentialize gender.

Since the publication of *Babbling Corpse*, vaporwave has endured a fair share of criticism. Most of the criticism, it seems, stems from a failure to define what vaporwave is. Search for it on most social media platforms and you will get a mix of retro aesthetics with no definable thread. Is an image of the Windows 98 logo "vaporwave"? Or a digital rendering of a sunset and palm trees against a vaguely 80s light grid?

Often vaporwave is conflated with synthwave, another internet-born genre that appeared online in the early 2010s and has since bubbled into the mainstream. Synthwave is defined by its naked embrace of 80s aesthetics: arpeggiated synths, jazzercise beats, saxophone, soaring vocals. Dua Lipa and the Weeknd have produced synthwave albums, and the soundtrack to the Netflix series *Stranger Things* is pure synthwave. Synthwave is less surreal than vaporwave, more high-definition; less like Negativland, more like "The Boys of Summer." If vaporwave is the viral ghost sent back in time to haunt the Reagan era, synthwave is the computer programmer trying to code that era back into existence.

Vaporwave is sometimes the label applied to "slowed + reverb" remixes. As the moniker makes obvious, these songs have been slowed down and treated with a light dose of reverb to give them a hazy, trippy vibe. Slowed + reverb remixing has been criticized as a gentrification of chopped and screwed, the production technique pioneered by DJ Screw in 1990s Houston. Whatever slowed + reverb is, it bears little resemblance to vaporwave, the best of which is beatless, looping, hallucinatory. Defining vaporwave as slowed + reverb is like defining rock and roll as 4/4 beats with guitars. And anything can be slowed and reverbed, including the most popular blockbuster singles of the present day. Vaporwave is uninterested in such obvious source material. It prefers to plunder the chintzy past with its malls and piped-in muzak, not the big-budget artists of today.

There have been moral panics about vaporwave being an essentially fascist genre of music. The "fashwave" subgenre celebrates neo-Nazis and far-right demagogues like Mussolini and Trump, set to motorik beats and arpeggiators. But fashwave is a subgenre of synthwave, not vaporwave. Certain aesthetic elements of vaporwave might get appropriated in fashwave, like images of Roman busts, but that doesn't mean vaporwave will radicalize anyone to become a reactionary nationalist. And even though synthwave can often be uncritical and unreflective, it too isn't inherently fascist.

Over the years, I've had to begrudgingly define vaporwave to keep at bay the critiques of essentialism: that vaporwave is essentially fascist, that it's essentially Marxist, and so forth. It isn't essentially anything. Its aesthetic markers might lend itself to certain readings, just as the blatant appeals to strongmen in fashwave can be read as obvious celebrations of war criminals. There can be different interpretations of vaporwave, but these aren't totally random. Vaporwave invites Marxist and political economy interpretations because of its production techniques, iconography, sound, feel, and mood. It is a psychedelic reframing of the songs of capital, once meant to anesthetize laborers and shoppers. Given the vaporwave treatment, these sounds take on a new life, perhaps as something strangely beautiful, haunting yet euphoric. This book is my interpretation of vaporwave as a genre replicating the weird experience of moving through an environment built for private consumption, from the airport to the mall.

Perhaps one day vaporwave won't make sense anymore. Although plenty of people still pass through airports and grocery stores, the act of going to a physical location to shop is now being replaced by delivery services. One can work from home and have their goods delivered by an underpaid "essential worker," who is watched by a smart doorbell as they drop off Amazon packages. No longer drifting through the mall, we scroll through lists instead: social media posts, Amazon wish lists, news headlines. Accompanying this activity is a new kind of muzak, the sound of a Spotify playlist tuned to our mood while collecting information about our every click, or an artificial intelligence-generated voice replicating the vocal characteristics of a cartoon character singing any number of hit singles. How might vaporwave reframe this new era of consumption and algorithmic weirding?

Looking back, the early 2010s seem almost unfamiliar to us. There is no shortage of mainstream protest music in the 2020s, and vaporwave is no longer a niche genre. Where news outlets once asked where the protest music is, NPR deemed 2020 "The Year of Protest Music" and published a playlist of songs by Lil Baby, Noname, Tyler Childers, and others. The era of the TED Talk and the "gee whiz" embrace of viral memes ended with the publication of Kevin Allocca's 2018 book, *Videocracy: How YouTube Is Changing The World ... With Double Rainbows, Singing Foxes, and Other Trends We Can't Stop Watching*. The book upon publication was an anachronism. By 2018, YouTube had already been excoriated for recommending pro-anorexia, conspiracy theory, anti-Semitic, and bizarre children's videos to viewers. None of these troubling algorithmic issues are mentioned in *Videocracy*, nor is there a single mention of content moderation, a job so awful that some moderators have sued the major platforms after developing post-traumatic stress disorder. These issues aren't mentioned in *Videocracy* because the book is a front for YouTube. It is a three-hundred-page form of promotional copy for the company to direct attention away from its reactionary tendencies and to the good old days of the 2010s, when charismatic white men on large stages convinced the Recession-weary public that social media could make anyone famous overnight.

Our time has its share of injustices, and just because famous celebrities signal their commitment to social justice, that doesn't mean we've entered into some better, freer world. Many things have worsened. Gratefully, though, the backlash against Big Tech is starting conversations about surveillance, algorithmic racism, and the environment — all topics that were being researched by trailblazing scholars long before *Videocracy* was published. Far from democratizing the world, platform capitalism is eroding democracy. It is a slow process, imperceptible most of the time until flashes of violence awaken us to what is happening. It is like global warming: you might not be able to see it all of the time, but it's happening. *Babbling Corpse* is a rebuke of a time when tech corporations engineered the mass delusion that society could be run by machines in the name of human freedom. It is also a reminder that we're still living under the spell.

Acknowledgments

The writing of this book could not have come at a more precarious period in my life, and many people were involved in helping me through the creative process. To these people I am forever grateful. The germ of this project was formed in Richard Menke's course on media theory at the University of Georgia. I took this class as an undergraduate at UGA and learned the fundamentals of media historiography and theory. Dr. Menke was the first to introduce me to the work being done on haunted media, which profoundly influenced this book. Esra Santesso and Christopher Sieving guided me through my final years as an undergraduate and encouraged me to tackle this book. They are all vastly important to me as scholars and mentors.

Reading the words of Mark Fisher for the first time ignited in me a fire for teaching others about Western politics and culture. His work on capitalism, hauntology, and depression challenged and energized me in ways few writers have. I am also indebted to Dominic Pettman, who gave me crucial advice.

My friends are all expert conversationalists, and talking through my ideas with them formed the structure of this book. Among those I would like to thank are Justin Belk, Michael Buice, Bobby Ferguson, Cory Jasin, Perry Lee, Dillon McCabe, Nick Malloy, Andrew Mines, Greg Moyer, JJ Posway, Kai Riedl, Philip Spence, Rachel Stoker, Chisolm Thompson, and Evan Tyor.

This book would not exist without the support from my parents and my two sisters. Thank you for encouraging me through the hardest parts of the past year and for teaching me to seek out knowledge on my own.

My center is Anna. She is my guide through the darkness.

Notes

Epigraphs

1. Jeffrey Sconce, *Haunted Media: Electronic Presence from Telegraphy to Television* (Durham, NC: Duke University Press, 2000), 170–171.
2. Terrance Hayes, "Buy One, Get One," in *Muscular Music* (Pittsburgh, PA: Carnegie Mellon University Press, 2006), 27.

Chapter 1

1. Samuel Taylor Coleridge, "The Rime of the Ancient Mariner," in *The Best Poems of the English Language: From Chaucer Through Frost*, ed. Harold Bloom (New York: HarperCollins Publishers, 2004), 368.
2. Jeffrey Sconce, *Haunted Media: Electronic Presence from Telegraphy to Television* (Durham, NC: Duke University Press, 2000), 2.
3. Ibid., 4.
4. Ibid., 127.
5. Ibid., 4.
6. Linda Badley, *Film, Horror, and the Body Fantastic* (Westport, CT: Greenwood Press, 1995), 42.
7. Sigmund Freud, *The Uncanny*, trans. David McLintock (New York: Penguin, 2003), 124.
8. David Toop, *Sinister Resonance: The Mediumship of the Listener* (New York: Continuum, 2010), 148.
9. Dylan Trigg, *The Memory of Place: A Phenomenology of the Uncanny* (Athens, OH: Ohio University Press, 2012), 26.
10. Ibid., 25–26.
11. Ibid., 27.
12. Ibid.
13. Don DeLillo, *White Noise* (New York: Penguin, 1986), 104.
14. Sconce, *Haunted Media*, 127.

15. Badley, *Film, Horror, and the Body Fantastic*, 42.
16. Simon Reynolds, *Retromania: Pop Culture's Addiction to Its Own Past* (New York: Faber and Faber, Inc., 2011), 314.
17. Marshall McLuhan, *Understanding Media: The Extensions of Man* (Cambridge, MA: MIT, 1994), 283.
18. Elizabeth Hellmuth Margulis, *On Repeat: How Music Plays the Mind* (New York: Oxford University Press, 2014), 84.
19. Ibid.
20. Reynolds, *Retromania*, 323.
21. Torben Sangild, "Glitch – The Beauty of Malfunction," in *Bad Music: The Music We Love to Hate*, eds. Christopher J. Washburne and Maiken Derno (New York: Routledge, 2004), 258-259.
22. Ibid., 267.
23. Reynolds, *Retromania*, 343–344.
24. Janne Vanhanen, "Loving the Ghost in the Machine: Aesthetics of Interruption," *CTheory*, November 26, 2001, http://www.ctheory.net/articles.aspx?id=312.
25. Ibid.

Chapter 2

1. Giacomo Leopardi, "Dialogue Between Nature and an Icelander," in *Dialogue Between Fashion and Death*, trans. Giovanni Cecchetti (New York: Penguin, 2010), 39.
2. Irmgard Emmelhainz, "Conditions of Visuality Under the Anthropocene and Images of the Anthropocene to Come," *e-flux*, 2015, http://www.e-flux.com/journal/conditions-of-visuality-under-the-anthropocene-and-images-of-the-anthropocene-to-come/.
3. Steven Shaviro, *The Universe of Things: On Speculative Realism* (Minneapolis, MN: University of Minnesota Press, 2014), 6.
4. "In The Dust Of This Planet" (2014), podcast radio program, *Radiolab*, Jad Abumrad, New York City. Available from:

http://www.radiolab.org/story/dust-planet/ (Accessed September 9, 2014).

5. Ibid.

6. Ibid.

7. "The Long Bright Dark," *True Detective*, Cary Joji Fukunaga, HBO, 2014, HBO Go.

8. Eugene Thacker, *In the Dust of This Planet: Horror of Philosophy vol. 1* (Winchester, UK: Zero, 2011), 1.

9. H.P. Lovecraft, "The Call of Cthulhu," in *The Call of Cthulhu and Other Weird Stories* (New York: Penguin, 1999), 139.

10. Trigg, *The Memory of Place*, 29.

11. Ibid.

12. Noël Carroll, "Horror and Humor," *The Journal of Aesthetics and Art Criticism* (1999): 146, *JSTOR Journals*, January 14, 2015.

13. Ibid., 155.

14. Michael Wesch, "Comments of the Electronic Frontier Foundation," *Electronic Frontier Foundation*, 2011, https://www.eff.org/files/filenode/2012_dmca_exemption_requests_final_1.pdf.

15. The CNN parody video is available here: http://nymag.com/daily/intelligencer/2015/03/cnn-made-a-2016-version-of-too-many-cooks.html.

16. Radiohead, "Idioteque," by Radiohead, Paul Lansky, and Arthur Kreiger, *Kid A* (Parlophone, 2000), CD.

Chapter 3

1. *Peter Pan*, Clyde Geronimi, Wilfred Jackson, Hamilton Luske, Walt Disney Productions, 1953.

2. Mark Fisher, *Capitalist Realism: Is There No Alternative?* (Winchester, UK: Zero, 2009), 39.

3. Fredric Jameson, "Postmodernism and Consumer Society," in *Critical Visions in Film Theory*, eds. Timothy Corrigan, Patricia White, and Meta Mazaj (Boston: Bedford/St. Martin's, 2011), 1036.

4. Jacques Derrida, *Specters of Marx: The State of the Debt, the Work of Mourning & the New International* (New York; London: Routledge, 2006), 45.

5. Jameson, "Postmodernism and Consumer Society," 1034.

6. Ibid., 1035.

7. Ibid.

8. Linda Hutcheon, *The Politics of Postmodernism* (London; New York: Routledge, 1993), 107.

9. Ibid., 113.

10. Jameson, "Postmodernism and Consumer Society," 1037.

11. Ibid., 1038.

12. Hutcheon, *The Politics of Postmodernism*, 114.

13. Jameson, "Postmodernism and Consumer Society," 1034.

14. Hutcheon, *The Politics of Postmodernism*, 119.

15. Jameson, "Postmodernism and Consumer Society," 1038.

16. Ibid., 1036.

17. Ibid., 1034.

18. Derrida, *Specters of Marx*, 11.

19. Ibid., 5.

20. Ibid., 106.

21. Mark Fisher, "What Is Hauntology?," in *Film Quarterly* 1 (2012): 20, *JSTOR Arts & Sciences III*, November 2013.

22. Ibid.

23. Ibid., 19.

24. Joseph Lanza, *Elevator Music: A Surreal History of Muzak, Easy-Listening, and Other Moodsong* (Ann Arbor, MI: University of Michigan Press, 2004), 4.

25. Ibid., 5.

26. Ibid., 17.

27. Ibid., 209.

28. Ibid., 150–152.

29. Ibid., 228.

30. Adam Harper, "Comment: Vaporwave and the pop-art of the virtual plaza," *Dummy*, July 12, 2012,

http://www.dummymag.com/features/adam-harper-vapor wave.
31. Personal email communication with the founder of SPF420, November 2, 2014. Name withheld.
32. Ibid.
33. Personal email communication with Ramona Xavier, November 2, 2014.
34. Adam Downer, review of *FLORAL SHOPPE* by MACINTOSH PLUS, Sputnikmusic, February 16, 2014, http://www.sputnikmusic.com/review/61016/Macintosh-Plus-FLORAL-SHOPPE/.
35. Xavier.
36. Ibid.
37. Mark Fisher, *Capitalist Realism: Is There No Alternative?* (Winchester, UK: Zero, 2009), 5.
38. Xavier.

Chapter 4

1. John Gray, *The Soul of the Marionette: A Short Inquiry Into Human Freedom* (New York: Farrar, Straus, and Giroux, 2015), 99.
2. Arcade Fire, "My Body is a Cage," by Arcade Fire, *Neon Bible* (Merge, 2007), CD.
3. Jennifer Egan, *A Visit from the Goon Squad* (New York: Random House, 2010), 203.
4. Naomi Klein, *The Shock Doctrine: The Rise of Disaster Capitalism* (New York: Picador, 2008), 20.
5. Slavoj Zizek, *Welcome to the Desert of the Real: Five Essays on September 11 and Related Dates* (London: Verso, 2012), 5–6.
6. Ibid., 55–56.
7. Ibid., 56.
8. Ibid.
9. Ibid., 45–46.

10. Simon Reynolds, *Retromania: Pop Culture's Addiction to Its Own Past* (New York: Faber and Faber, Inc., 2011), 57.

11. Ibid., 71.

12. qtd. in Andrew Keen, *The Internet is Not the Answer* (New York: Atlantic Monthly Press, 2015), 138.

13. Reynolds, *Retromania*, 110.

14. See Nicholas Carr's *The Shallows: What the Internet is Doing to Our Brains* (New York: W.W. Norton, 2011).

15. Reynolds, *Retromania*, 73.

16. Ibid., 120–121.

17. Ibid., 122.

18. Ibid., 425–426.

19. Stuart Kelly, "Alan Moore: 'Why shouldn't you have a bit of fun while dealing with the deepest issues of the mind?'", *The Guardian*, November 22, 2013, http://www.theguardian.com/books/2013/nov/22/alan-moore-comic-books-interview.

20. Chris Hedges, *Wages of Rebellion* (New York: Nation Books, 2015), 33.

21. Adam Harper, "Comment: Vaporwave and the pop-art of the virtual plaza," *Dummy*, July 12, 2012, http://www.dummymag.com/features/adam-harper-vaporwave.

22. Ibid., "Comment: 'Distroid – the muscular music of hi-def doom," *Dummy*, July 13, 2012, http://www.dummymag.com/Features/distroid-gatekeeper-fatima-al-qadiri-adam-harper.

23. Ibid.

24. Ibid.

25. Russell Thomas, "Interview: Dream Catalogue's Hong Kong Express on Vaporwave's Past, Present, and Future," *Red Bull Music Academy Daily*, September 8, 2014, http://daily.redbullmusicacademy.com/2014/09/dream-catalogue-interview.

26. Ibid.
27. Stephen Thompson, "The Good Listener: Do You Ever Just Get Sick of Music?", *NPR*, September 13, 2014, http://www.npr.org/sections/allsongs/2014/09/12/348019155/the-good-listener-do-you-ever-just-get-sick-of-music.
28. Lindsay Zoladz, "Everything Happens So Much," Pitchfork, August 6, 2014, http://pitchfork.com/features/ordinary-machines/9474-every thing-happens-so-much/.
29. Ruth Singleton, review of *An Awesome Wave* by alt-J, Drowned in Sound, May 28, 2012, http://drownedinsound.com/releases/17093/reviews/41451 41.
30. Jenny Stevens, review of *An Awesome Wave* by alt-J, *New Musical Express*, May 25, 2012, http://www.nme.com/reviews/alt-j/13233.
31. Jen Long, review of *An Awesome Wave* by alt-J, BBC Music, 2012, http://www.bbc.co.uk/music/reviews/mvm5.
32. Laura Snapes, review of *An Awesome Wave* by alt-J, Pitchfork, September 28, 2012, http://pitchfork.com/reviews/albums/17233-an-awesome-wave/.
33. Ian Cohen, review of *This Is All Yours* by alt-J, Pitchfork, September 23, 2014, http://pitchfork.com/reviews/albums/19843-alt-j-this-is-all-yours/.
34. Chart history for *This Is All Yours* by alt-J, http://www.billboard.com/artist/278723/Alt-J/chart?f=794.
35. Lyrics heard on "Every Other Freckle" and "Fitzpleasure" by alt-J.
36. Lyrics heard on "God Made Girls" by RaeLynn.
37. James Parker and Nicholas Croggon, "The Trouble with Contemporary Music Criticism: Retromania, Retro-historicism, and History," Tiny Mix Tapes, January 2014,

http://www.tinymixtapes.com/features/the-trouble-with-contemporary-music-criticism.

38. Ibid.
39. Ibid.
40. Ibid.
41. Chris Richards, "Taylor Swift's '1989': A pivot into pop, a misstep into conformity," *The Washington Post*, October 27, 2014,
https://www.washingtonpost.com/news/style-blog/wp/2014/10/27/taylor-swifts-1989-a-pivot-into-pop-a-misstep-into-conformity/.
42. Ibid.
43. Ryan Alexander Diduck, "We Are All Freemans: Pop Culture and Future Reckonings in 2014," *The Quietus*, December 8, 2014,
http://thequietus.com/articles/16859-we-are-all-freemans-future-surveillance-pop-culture-2014-wreath-lecture.
44. William Kremer and Claudia Hammond, "Hikikomori: Why are so many Japanese men refusing to leave their rooms?," BBC News, July 5, 2013,
http://www.bbc.com/news/magazine-23182523.
45. Look at the fashion phenomenon, normcore, as an indication of our culture – especially the left-leaning, city-dwelling youth culture – realizing its placelessness in a world that dooms it to a future not worth anticipating. "The Internet and globalization have challenged the myth of individuality (we are all one in 7 billion), while making connecting with others easier than ever," writes journalist Fiona Duncan, categorizing normcore as the fashion statement that emphasizes our loss of individuality and our coming to terms with a failed future ("Normcore: Fashion for Those Who Realize They're One in 7 Billion," NYmag.com, February 26, 2014,

http://nymag.com/thecut/2014/02/normcore-fashion-trend. html). The fad is comprised of throwaway 90s-wear inspired partly by the clothes worn by the cast of Seinfeld or perhaps the tourist look of New York City-based musician Devonte Hynes – poor-fitting turtlenecks, boxy Levi's, chunky white Nikes, primary colors, overalls.

By early 2015, normcore, the logical conclusion to a hipster culture that had slowly voided irony of its sting throughout the 2010s, collapsed on itself with the rise of fashionable sweatpants and joggers, often sold in "fast fashion" shops such as H&M and Topshop. The fad spread quickly, and soon even big-box retailers like Target were carrying joggers of all colors. These are not only clothes that ease you of the burden of individuality in a globalized world; they are clothes you could wear on your sofa binging on Netflix, or that you could wear out to the bar, or to the grocery store, or anywhere essentially because they are comfortable and – most importantly – they are just *easy to wear*. They don't impress themselves upon you. They don't interrupt you or remind you they're there. They're more "uniform" than exercise apparel. They're cheap to make in an overseas sweatshop and easy to wear in front of a computer screen all day.

At this point it's only fitting to consult one of the icons of normcore before there was such a word – Jerry Seinfeld. In the *Seinfeld* episode "The Pilot," Jerry sees his friend George Costanza has taken to wearing sweatpants, and his reaction is completely out of step with our current fashion climate. "You know the message you're sending out to the world with these sweatpants?" Jerry asks George. "You're telling the world, 'I give up. I can't compete in normal society. I'm miserable, so I might as well be comfortable.'"

Might as well, right? And by the looks of normcore and fashionable joggers, then, we're settling in for a long stretch of playing up the notion that we are nothing in this world, while wearing our pajamas to work in a desperate attempt to fulfill the consumerist maxim – feel good all the time.

Bibliography

Badley, Linda. *Film, Horror, and the Body Fantastic*. Westport, CT: Greenwood, 1995.

DeLillo, Don. *White Noise*. New York: Penguin, 1986.

Derrida, Jacques. *Specters of Marx: The State of the Debt, the Work of Mourning & the New International*. New York; London: Routledge, 2006.

Egan, Jennifer. *A Visit from the Goon Squad*. New York: Random House, 2010.

Fisher, Mark. *Capitalist Realism: Is There No Alternative?* Winchester, UK: Zero, 2009.

Freud, Sigmund. *The Uncanny*. Trans. David McLintock. New York: Penguin, 2003.

Gray, John. *The Soul of the Marionette: A Short Inquiry Into Human Freedom*. New York: Farrar, Straus, and Giroux, 2015.

Hayes, Terrance. "Buy One, Get One." *Muscular Music*. Pittsburgh, PA: Carnegie Mellon University Press, 2006.

Hedges, Chris. *Wages of Rebellion*. New York: Nation Books, 2015.

Hutcheon, Linda. *The Politics of Postmodernism*. London; New York: Routledge, 1993.

Jameson, Fredric. "Postmodernism and Consumer Society." *Critical Visions in Film Theory*. Eds. Timothy Corrigan, Patricia White, and Meta Mazaj. Boston: Bedford/St. Martin's, 2011.

Keen, Andrew. *The Internet is Not the Answer*. New York: Atlantic Monthly Press, 2015.

Klein, Naomi. *The Shock Doctrine: The Rise of Disaster Capitalism*. New York: Picador, 2008.

Lanza, Joseph. *Elevator Music: A Surreal History of Muzak, Easy-Listening, and Other Moodsong*. Ann Arbor, MI: University of Michigan Press, 2004.

Leopardi, Giacomo. "Dialogue Between Nature and an Icelander." *Dialogue Between Fashion and Death*. Trans. Giovanni Cecchetti. New York: Penguin, 2010.

Lovecraft, H.P. "The Call of Cthulhu." *The Call of Cthulhu and Other Weird Stories*. New York: Penguin, 1999.

McLuhan, Marshall. *Understanding Media: The Extensions of Man*. Cambridge, MA: MIT, 1994.

Margulis, Elizabeth Hellmuth. *On Repeat: How Music Plays the Mind*. New York: Oxford University Press, 2014.

Reynolds, Simon. *Retromania: Pop Culture's Addiction to Its Own Past*. New York: Faber and Faber, Inc., 2011.

Sangild, Torben. "Glitch – The Beauty of Malfunction." *Bad Music: The Music We Love to Hate*. Eds. Christopher J. Washburne and Maiken Derno. New York: Routledge, 2004.

Sconce, Jeffrey. *Haunted Media: Electronic Presence from Telegraphy to Television*. Durham, NC: Duke UP, 2000.

Shaviro, Steven. *The Universe of Things: On Speculative Realism*. Minneapolis, MN: University of Minnesota Press, 2014.

Thacker, Eugene. *In the Dust of This Planet: Horror of Philosophy vol. 1*. Winchester, UK: Zero, 2011.

Toop, David. *Sinister Resonance: The Mediumship of the Listener*. London: Continuum, 2011.

Trigg, Dylan. *The Memory of Place: A Phenomenology of the Uncanny*. Athens: Ohio UP, 2012.

Zizek, Slavoj. *Welcome to the Desert of the Real: Five Essays on September 11 and Related Dates*. London: Verso, 2012.

Discography

alt-J, *This Is All Yours* (Infectious, 2014).

Bebetune$, *Inhale C-4 $$$$$* (self-released, 2011).

Bodyguard, *Silica Gel* (self-released, 2012).

Brandon Flowers, *The Desired Effect* (Island, 2015).

The Caretaker, *An Empty Bliss Beyond this World* (self-released, 2011).

——, *Selected Memories from the Haunted Ballroom* (self-released, 1999).

Chuck Person, *Chuck Person's Eccojams Vol. 1* (self-released, 2010).

Death Grips, *Government Plates* (Third Worlds and Harvest, 2013).

esc 不在, *Black Horse* (self-released, 2011).

g h o s t i n g, *Telenights* (Dream Catalogue, 2014).

Internet Club, *Vanishing Vision* (self-released, 2012).

James Ferraro, *Far Side Virtual* (Hippos in Tanks, 2011).

John Oswald, *Plunderphonics 69/96* (Fony and Seeland, 2001).

Local News, *Ghost Broadcast* (self-released, 2013).

Macintosh Plus, *Floral Shoppe* (Beer on the Rug, 2011).

Miami Vice, *Culture Island* (self-released, 2012).

Midnight Television, *Midnight Television* (Beer on the Rug, 2011).

Negativland, *U2 EP* (SST and Seeland, 1991).

New Dreams Ltd Initiation Tape, *Part One* (self-released, 2011).

Oneohtrix Point Never, *R Plus Seven* (Warp, 2013).

Principles, *Candy Brain* (Alianthus Recordings, 2013).

Taylor Swift, *1989* (Big Machine, 2014).

Topographic Maps, *Tropical Disturbances* (Alianthus Recordings, 2011).

Transilvanian Hunger, 葛城 ミサト (self-released, 2013).

情報デスクVIRTUAL, 札幌コンテンポラリー (Beer on the Rug, 2012).

18 Carat Affair, *Televised Tragedies* (self-released, 2011).

CULTURE, SOCIETY & POLITICS

Contemporary culture has eliminated the concept and public figure of the intellectual. A cretinous anti-intellectualism presides, cheer-led by hacks in the pay of multinational corporations who reassure their bored readers that there is no need to rouse themselves from their stupor. Zer0 Books knows that another kind of discourse - intellectual without being academic, popular without being populist - is not only possible: it is already flourishing. Zer0 is convinced that in the unthinking, blandly consensual culture in which we live, critical and engaged theoretical reflection is more important than ever before.

If you have enjoyed this book, why not tell other readers by posting a review on your preferred book site.

You may also wish to
subscribe to our Zer0 Books YouTube Channel.

Bestsellers from Zer0 Books include:

Poor but Sexy
Culture Clashes in Europe East and West
Agata Pyzik
How the East stayed East and the West stayed West.
Paperback: 978-1-78099-394-2 ebook: 978-1-78099-395-9

An Anthropology of Nothing in Particular
Martin Demant Frederiksen
A journey into the social lives of meaninglessness.
Paperback: 978-1-78535-699-5 ebook: 978-1-78535-700-8

In the Dust of This Planet
Horror of Philosophy vol. 1
Eugene Thacker
In the first of a series of three books on the Horror of Philosophy,
In the Dust of This Planet offers the genre of horror as a way of
thinking about the unthinkable.
Paperback: 978-1-84694-676-9 ebook: 978-1-78099-010-1

The End of Oulipo?
An Attempt to Exhaust a Movement
Lauren Elkin, Veronica Esposito
Paperback: 978-1-78099-655-4 ebook: 978-1-78099-656-1

Capitalist Realism
Is There No Alternative?
Mark Fisher
An analysis of the ways in which capitalism has presented
itself as the only realistic political-economic system.
Paperback: 978-1-84694-317-1 ebook: 978-1-78099-734-6

Rebel Rebel
Chris O'Leary
David Bowie: every single song. Everything you
want to know, everything you didn't know.
Paperback: 978-1-78099-244-0 ebook: 978-1-78099-713-1

Cartographies of the Absolute
Alberto Toscano, Jeff Kinkle
An aesthetics of the economy for the twenty-first century.
Paperback: 978-1-78099-275-4 ebook: 978-1-78279-973-3

Malign Velocities
Accelerationism and Capitalism
Benjamin Noys
Long listed for the Bread and Roses Prize 2015, *Malign Velocities*
argues against the need for speed, tracking acceleration
as the symptom of the ongoing crises of capitalism.
Paperback: 978-1-78279-300-7 ebook: 978-1-78279-299-4

Babbling Corpse
Vaporwave and the Commodification of Ghosts
Grafton Tanner
Paperback: 978-1-78279-759-3 ebook: 978-1-78279-760-9

New Work New Culture
Work we want and a culture that strengthens us
Frithjof Bergmann
A serious alternative for mankind and the planet.
Paperback: 978-1-78904-064-7 ebook: 978-1-78904-065-4

Romeo and Juliet in Palestine
Teaching Under Occupation
Tom Sperlinger
Life in the West Bank, the nature of pedagogy and
the role of a university under occupation.
Paperback: 978-1-78279-637-4 ebook: 978-1-78279-636-7

Color, Facture, Art and Design
Iona Singh
This materialist definition of fine-art develops
guidelines for architecture, design, cultural-studies
and ultimately social change.
Paperback: 978-1-78099-629-5 ebook: 978-1-78099-630-1

Sweetening the Pill
or How We Got Hooked on Hormonal Birth Control
Holly Grigg-Spall
Has contraception liberated or oppressed women?
Sweetening the Pill breaks the silence on the dark side
of hormonal contraception.
Paperback: 978-1-78099-607-3 ebook: 978-1-78099-608-0

Why Are We The Good Guys?
Reclaiming Your Mind from the Delusions of Propaganda
David Cromwell
A provocative challenge to the standard ideology that
Western power is a benevolent force in the world.
Paperback: 978-1-78099-365-2 ebook: 978-1-78099-366-9

The Writing on the Wall
On the Decomposition of Capitalism and its Critics
Anselm Jappe, Alastair Hemmens
A new approach to the meaning of social emancipation.
Paperback: 978-1-78535-581-3 ebook: 978-1-78535-582-0

Neglected or Misunderstood
The Radical Feminism of Shulamith Firestone
Victoria Margree
An interrogation of issues surrounding gender, biology,
sexuality, work and technology, and the ways in which our
imaginations continue to be in thrall to ideologies of
maternity and the nuclear family.
Paperback: 978-1-78535-539-4 ebook: 978-1-78535-540-0

How to Dismantle the NHS in 10 Easy Steps (Second Edition)
Youssef El-Gingihy
The story of how your NHS was sold off and why you will have
to buy private health insurance soon. A new expanded second
edition with chapters on junior doctors' strikes and government
blueprints for US-style healthcare.
Paperback: 978-1-78904-178-1 ebook: 978-1-78904-179-8

Digesting Recipes
The Art of Culinary Notation
Susannah Worth
A recipe is an instruction, the imperative tone of the expert,
but this constraint can offer its own kind of potential. A recipe
need not be a domestic trap but might instead offer escape –
something to fantasise about or aspire to.

Paperback: 978-1-78279-860-6 ebook: 978-1-78279-859-0

Most titles are published in paperback and as an ebook.
Paperbacks are available in traditional bookshops. Both print
and ebook formats are available online.
Follow us at:
facebook.com/ZeroBooks
twitter.com/Zer0Books
instagram.com/zero.books